This b

بسم الله الرحمن الرحيم

When Allah desires good for a servant,
He gives him understanding of the religion.
—Prophetic Tradition

Al-Nawawī's Manual of Islam

Translated by

NUH HA MIM KELLER

The Islamic Texts Society

First published in U.S.A. 1994.
This U.K. edition published 1996 by
The Islamic Texts Society
22a Brooklands Avenue
Cambridge, CB2 2DQ, U.K.

ISBN 0 946621 54 3 *paper*

British Library Cataloguing in Publication Data
A catalogue record of this book is available from
The British Library

Arabic calligraphy by the Syrian calligrapher Salih Nasab,
except for the Basmalah facing the title page,
which is by the Turkish master Hamid Aytaç.

Printed in Egypt

CONTENTS

In the name of Allah
Most Merciful and Compassionate

INTRODUCTION

Praise to Allah Most High, who shows whomever He wills the path to eternal happiness, the sunna of His beloved prophet (Allah bless him and give him peace), to whom He gave the message for mankind:

"Say: 'If you love Allah, then follow me; Allah will love you and forgive you your sins. Verily Allah is forgiving and compassionate'" (Koran 3:31).

To *follow* the Prophet (Allah bless him and give him peace) was a simple matter for his Companions (Sahaba); they knew and loved him, and when he would tell them something, they said, "We hear and obey." When he passed from this world, the Koranic imperative remained, and the Companions diligently preserved all that they had learned from him, both the Divine Book that Allah had sent with him, and his example, in word and deed. Those who had taken knowledge from him during his lifetime passed it on to those after them, and so on down to our own times—and little wonder, for in their eyes, these were medicines that meant eternal life for whoever possessed them.

The Koran, the first source of guidance, was memorized during the lifetime of the Prophet (Allah bless him and give him peace) by thousands of Companions in a deliberate and sustained educational effort centered around the mosque in Medina, whence teachers were sent to tribes in all parts of the Arabian Peninsula. The *hadith*s, or eyewitness accounts of the Prophet's words and deeds, were transmitted in precisely the same way, first to contemporaries and then to subsequent generations. Someone who has lived among the Arabs can attest to their phenomenal powers of memory, and it is not difficult to understand why, given their concern, the individually recorded reports from his life came to number over a hundred thousand. Many of these were from various narrators describing the same events, but allowing for repetitions (which were carefully memorized and transmitted by hadith masters (huffaz)), and discounting spurious (mawdu‘) accounts by later narrators (which were equally carefully preserved, so as not to be accepted), the substantive hadiths that reached the Muslims from the Prophet (Allah bless him and give him peace) numbered approximately thirty thousand.

The Muslim community responded to the magnitude of this knowledge and to the ethical imperative of living it on a daily basis with a wide range of scholarly disciplines that furnished the means to distill this vast tradition into a clear, practical answer to the question: What does Allah expect of one?

This then, is the basis of the study of Sacred Law or *Shari‘a* in Islam: we have been ordered to follow the Prophet (Allah bless him and give him peace), and he is no longer alive to personally teach us. All that has reached us of it has reached us through men. And this is why Muslims from earliest times have relied on the most knowledgeable of these men to take their religion from—whether in hadith, tenets of faith (‘aqida), Koranic exegesis (tafsir), or the other Islamic sciences. The foremost of them were termed *Imam*s or "leaders," in view of their position in each field, so their knowledge could be accepted and followed.

For orthodox Muslims (Ahl al-Sunna wa al-Jama‘a), there are four Imams of Sacred Law: Abu Hanifa, Malik, Shafi‘i, and Ahmad. The rulings that they concur upon, about 75 percent of them, are a decisive proof for Sunni Muslims; while those they differ upon have been accepted by the Community for over a thousand years as a mercy from Allah. Whoever examines the differences, moreover, finds that their roots invariably extend back to the prophetic Companions, from whom the Imams took their knowledge in an unbroken series of masters, the Companions in turn having been educated by the Prophet himself (Allah bless him and give him peace) such that it is unimaginable that their differences should be blameworthy.

Despite the preeminence of their rank, the Imams regarded themselves as explainers rather than legislators, and one of their greatest legacies was to the subsequent generations of scholars who followed in their footsteps, nearly a hundred in each school, scholars of the first rank who carefully rechecked the Imams' work in light of the primary texts of the Koran and hadith. The result was the traditional Islamic *Shari'a* or Sacred Law embodied in the four schools of jurisprudence, which has won acceptance among Sunni Muslims down to our own day and become the unconquerable fortress of orthodox Islam.

This Book

The author of the text, the thirteenth-century hadith specialist and jurisprudent Imam Nawawi, was among the intellectual heirs of Imam Shafi'i, whose work he refined until his books became references even more frequently used in the school than the early works of the Imam himself.

But with their scholarly excellence, many of Nawawi's books are lengthy and detailed, while for the purposes of the present volume, the translator sought a work whose small size would recommend itself to the needs contemporary users. Also, upon examining the short works of Sacred Law that exist, the translator found that the original reason that many of them were authored in their brevity was as an aid to students memorizing them, rather than to give Muslims a basic guide to the rules of Islam.

The two aims are not necessarily the same thing. In previous centuries, students would come from their villages or neighborhoods to sheikhs, who would have them memorize a *matn* or short basic text of fiqh (jurisprudence), then teach the students what the condensed and often technical language of the particular rulings implied, the conditions for applying them, their evidential bases from Koran and hadith, and so forth. In this way, students returning to their native places were able to give reliable answers based on qualified scholarship to most of the questions in Sacred Law they encountered (as the *matn*s memorized were comprehensive), and then go on to explain the details of them they had learned from their sheikhs.

With such educational interests in view, the first priority of a *matn*'s author was often to state the content as briefly as possible to facilitate memorizing. The present work, *al-Maqasid,* is such a *matn* and reflects this need, and we find in it, for example, that Imam Nawawi has summarized the prayer (salat) in a few brief lists of integrals, conditions, and sunnas, to enable students who learn them to answer a wide range of questions on whether a particular prayer is valid. By way of contrast, the present translation aims at teaching the prayer and other aspects of Islam to learners, and lists of elements do not suffice for this, but have to be supplemented with a fuller description, for readers who want to know how to pray step by step. The goal in rendering the present work has thus been to provide an English translation that combines the reliability of a famous fiqh *matn* with an explanative style that does not require a specialist to understand.

Some Points About the Book

The basic text, Imam Nawawi's *al-Maqasid: ma yajibu ma'rifatuhu min al din* [The objectives: what is necessary to know of the religion] (9.21) below has been filled out with interlineal notes from parallel sections of *The Reliance of the Traveller: A Classic Manual of Islamic Sacred Law* (9.13), a comprehensive textbook in Shafi'i jurisprudence recently published in English and Arabic, translated from Ahmad ibn Naqib al-Misri's *'Umdat al-salik* (9.17). *The Reliance of the Traveller* is particularly suited to explain *al-Maqasid* because it represents, as its author notes, the soundest positions of the Shafi'i school based on the recensions of Imam Nawawi and Imam Rafi'i, giving precedence to Nawawi because he is the foremost reference of the school.

In the texts below, commentary from *The Reliance of the Traveller* is distinguished from the text of *al-Maqasid* by parentheses, and is introduced in the English by a capital letter *R*. Remarks by the translator are similarly parenthesized but introduced with a lowercase *n*. Other notes begin with the author's name at the first of the quotation, and end with the source's title, volume, page number, and reference number from the present volume's bibliographical section 9; as in the preceding paragraph, where the reference number appears after each of the first three book titles.

The paragraphs of the text have been numbered to facilitate cross-reference, and titles and subtitles added by the translator. A small number of rulings have been omitted about matters deemed too rare to benefit most English-speaking Muslims (for example, zakat assessment on herds of camels). Within the rulings, columns of necessary *conditions* or *integrals,* meaning that all of them must be present for the ruling to hold true, are itemized by letters: (a), (b), (c), and so on. An example is the conditions for the validity of the prayer, which must all be met for the prayer to be valid. Columns of *examples* or instances of a ruling's applicability are itemized by numbers: (1), (2), (3), and so on, indicating that not all need exist, but any one of them suffices to apply the ruling, such as the things which invalidate fasting, the existence of any of which invalidates it.

Those who use the transliteration provided in the present volume to pronounce the Arabic of dhikr and supplications may also like to read or tape-record a native speaker reading the Arabic text indicated by the cross-reference number after each transliteration, directing the reader to section 10 at the end of the book.

Finally, a number of the notes of *The Reliance of the Traveller* have been appended to the end of the present volume to clarify certain points.

May Allah bless all who read this book with an increase of *baraka* and the love of Allah and His messenger (Allah bless him and give him peace) in this world and the next. Ameen.

ABBREVIATIONS

Ar. .... Arabic
ca. .... approximately
cm. ... centimeters
def: ... defined at another ruling
dis: ... discussed at another ruling
km. ... kilometers
lit. ..... literally
mi. .... miles
n: ...... remark by the translator
par. ... paragraph
pl. ..... plural
R: ..... from *The Reliance of the Traveller*

AUTHOR'S PREFACE

In the name of Allah, Most Merciful and Compassionate. Praise to Allah, Lord of the Worlds. The final outcome is to the pious, with enmity towards none save wrongdoers. And blessings and peace upon our liegelord Muhammad, the seal of the prophets and exemplar of the godfearing, and upon his folk and Companions one and all, those who followed after them, and all the righteous.

To commence, the following are beneficial objectives and resplendent lights: I ask Allah to make the work purely for His sake and to reward me for it out of His generosity. He is the protector of whoever seeks refuge in Him and takes by the hand whoever relies on Him. I have arranged them in seven sections.

1

FUNDAMENTALS OF FAITH AND SACRED LAW

أصول الدين

CONTENTS:

Tenets of Faith

1.1 The first obligation of all who are morally responsible (Ar. *mukallaf,* someone who has reached puberty and is of sound mind) is to know God, meaning to know that He is existent and not nonexistent; beginninglessly eternal, not originating in or subject to time or space; everlastingly abiding, not subject to end; dissimilar to and other than anything within time or space, nothing in any way resembling Him; self-subsistent, free of need for anything through which to exist or any determinant to condition Him; One, without co-sharer in His entity, attributes, or actions; possessed of almighty power, will, knowledge, life, hearing, sight, speech, such that He is almighty, and wills, knows, lives, hears, sees, and speaks.

1.2 He sent the prophets out of His generosity, protecting them from everything unbecoming them, guarding them from both lesser sins and enormities both before their prophethood and thereafter, and from every offensive physical trait such as leprosy or blindness, though they ate, drank, and married. They were the best of all created beings; and the highest of them was him whom Allah chose to be the final seal of prophethood, whose Sacred Law superseded all previously valid religious laws, our prophet Muhammad (Allah bless him and give him peace). His Companions (Sahaba) were the finest generation, the best of them being Abu Bakr, then 'Umar, then 'Uthman, then 'Ali, may the benefaction of Allah be upon them all.

1.3 We believe in everything that Allah has informed us of upon the tongue of Muhammad (Allah bless him and give him peace), such as the angels, the sacred scriptures, the questioning of the dead in their graves about their faith, the resurrection of the dead, their being gathered unto the Judgment Day, the terror of it, the taking of the pages in which one's good and bad deeds are recorded, the weighing of them, the balance scales, the high, narrow bridge over the hellfire that the saved will pass over to paradise, the intercession of the prophets and righteous for others, and in paradise and hell.

1.4 Everything that is necessarily known by Muslims to be of the religion (R: *necessarily known* meaning the things that any Muslim would know about if asked) is obligatory to believe, and anyone who denies it is a non-Muslim (kafir, dis: 8.1) (R: unless he is a recent convert or was born and raised in the wilderness or for some similar reason has been unable to learn his religion properly. Muslims in such a condition should be informed about the truth, and if they then continue as before, they are adjudged non-Muslims, as is also the case with any Muslim who believes it permissible to commit adultery, drink wine, kill without right, or do other acts that are necessarily known to be unlawful).

Fundamentals of Islam

1.5 The pillars of Islam consist of five things: to say the two Testifications of Faith: *Ash-hadu an lā ilāha illa Llāh(u), wa ash-hadu anna Muḥammadan Rasūlu Llāh* (10.1) ("I testify that there is no god but Allah and I testify that Muhammad is the Messenger of Allah") (R: even if they are not spoken in Arabic), without which one's Islam is not valid; the prayer (salat); zakat; the pilgrimage to Mecca; and fasting the month of Ramadan.

The preconditions for the validity of one's Islam are that one have reached puberty, be of sound mind, that the Prophet's message (Allah bless him and give him peace) have reached one, that one accept it voluntarily, and that one utter the two Testifications of Faith in their proper order without separating them, using the word *testify* in each. One must also know what is meant by them, and must acknowledge all that is necessarily known to be of the religion (def: 1.4) if one has denied any of it despite uttering them; and one must state them unequivocally.

1.6 The meaning of *true faith* (iman) is that one believes in Allah, His angels, His revealed books, His messengers, the Last Day, and in destiny, its good and evil.

1.7 Religion (din) consists of three matters: doing what Allah has commanded, avoiding what He has forbidden, and accepting what He has destined (dis: 8.2).

1.8 The foundations of the religion are four: the Koran, the sunna, scholarly consensus (ijma‘, (def: 8.3)), and analogy (qiyas, (8.11.b(III))) from other established rulings, when the latter two are recognized as binding by Islamic scholarship. Whatever contravenes these four bases is blameworthy innovation (bid‘a, def: 8.4), and its perpetrator is an innovator who Muslims are obliged to avoid the company of and rebuke.

The Sacred Law

1.9 The rulings of the Sacred Law are five: obligatory, recommended, unlawful, offensive, and permissible.

(1) The *obligatory* (wajib) is that whose performance is rewarded (n: by Allah in the next life) and whose nonperformance is punished.

(2) The *recommended* (mandub) is that whose performance is rewarded, but whose nonperformance is not punished.

(3) The *unlawful* (haram) is that whose nonperformance is rewarded and whose performance is punished.

(4) The *offensive* (makruh) is that whose nonperformance is rewarded but whose performance is not punished.

(5) The *permissible* (mubah) is that whose performance is not rewarded and whose nonperformance is not punished.

1.10 *Prescribed* (fard), *obligatory* (wajib), *mandatory* (muhattam), and *required* (lazim) all mean the same thing (n: i.e. (1) above), though the obligatory is distinguished into two categories, the personally obligatory and the communally obligatory.

(1) The *personally obligatory* (fard al-'ayn) is required from every morally responsible (def: 1.1) person individually, such that if someone performs it, the obligation of performing it is not lifted from others, as with the prescribed prayer (salat) or giving *zakat*.

(2) As for the *communally obligatory* (fard al-kifaya), it is that which if some do, the obligation is lifted from the rest, as with some member of a group returning a newcomer's greeting of "*as-Salāmu 'alaykum,*" or performing the funeral prayer, memorizing the Koran, commanding the right and forbidding the wrong when it is called for, or undertaking beneficial occupations that society needs.

1.11 The terms *sunna, recommended* (mandub), *preferable* (mustahabb), *meritorious* (fadila), and *desirable* (muraghghab fihi), all mean the same thing: that which the Prophet (Allah bless him and give him peace) said, or did (aside from what pertained to him alone (n: such as the night vigil (tahajjud) prayer, which was obligatory only for him)), or approved of in others, or accepted, or intended to do but did not carry out, as with fasting on 9 Muharram.

The Remembrance of Allah (Dhikr)

1.12 It is obligatory to say, *Ash-hadu an lā ilāh illa Llāhu wa ash-hadu anna Muḥammadan rasūlu Llāh* (10.2) ("I testify that there is no god but Allah and I testify that

Muhammad is the messenger of Allah") once in a lifetime, and it is highly desirable to do so frequently. It means that one acknowledges the oneness of Allah Most High, and the messengerhood of our liegelord Muhammad (Allah bless him and give him peace). (n: For a note on the transliterated Arabic of the present volume, see 8.5).

1.13 The best form of worship, next to having faith in the heart (iman), is the prayer (salat).

1.14 The best remembrance (dhikr) of Allah, next to recital of the Koran, is *Lā ilāha illa Llāh* (10.3) ("There is no god but Allah"), meaning no other in existence is worthy of worship besides Allah.

The best glorification of Allah Most High is *Subḥānaka lā nuḥṣī thanā'an 'alayka Anta kamā athnayta 'alā nafsik* (10.4) ("Exalted be You, we are unable to glorify You as You glorify Yourself").

The best praise is *al-Ḥamdu li Llāhi ḥamdan yuwāfī ni'amahu wa yukāfi'u mazīdah* (10.5) ("Praise be to Allah, in the measure of His blessings and commensurate with His increase of them").

The best form of blessings upon the Prophet (Allah bless him and give him peace) is *Allāhumma ṣalli 'alā Muḥammadin wa 'alā āli Muḥammadin kamā ṣallayta 'alā Ibrāhīma wa 'alā āli Ibrāhīm(a), wa bārik 'alā Muḥammadin wa 'alā āli Muḥammadin kamā barakta 'alā Ibrāhīma wa 'alā āli Ibrāhīma fī l-'ālamīna innaka ḥamīdun majīd* (10.6) ("O Allah, bless Muhammad and the folk of Muhammad as You blessed Ibrahim and the folk of Ibrahim. O Allah, show grace to Muhammad and the folk of Muhammad as You showed grace to Ibrahim and the folk of Ibrahim in the worlds; truly, You are the Most Praiseworthy and Noble"). This is called the "Perfect Blessing" or "Ibrahimic Blessing."

The blessing upon the Prophet (Allah bless him and give

him peace, and increase him in honor) is obligatory in the final Testification of Faith (Tashahhud) of the prayer. (n: Aside from the prayer,) some scholars hold that it is obligatory but once in a lifetime, while others say it is obligatory whenever the Prophet (Allah bless him and give him peace) is mentioned. Others hold it is obligatory at every gathering, while others hold otherwise.

The Righteous

1.15 One should believe in the closeness to Allah of whoever has Sacred Learning and lives it, who adheres to the prescribed manners of the Sacred Law and keeps the company of the righteous. As for the bereft of reason or deranged, like those overcome by the divine attraction (majdhub) without outward responsibility to obey the Sacred Law, we leave them be, consigning the knowledge of their real state to Allah, though it is obligatory to condemn whatever proceeds from them in contravention of the external appearances of the divine command, in observance of the rules of Sacred Law.

2

PURIFICATION

الطهارة

CONTENTS:

Purification

2.1 (R: *Purification* (tahara) in Sacred Law means lifting a state of *ritual impurity* (hadath, def: 2.8), removing *filth* (najasa, 2.3), or matters similar to these, such as a *purifica-*

tory bath (ghusl, 2.19) that is merely sunna, or renewing *ablution* (wudu, 2.10) when there has been no intervening ritual impurity.)

Water

2.2 Purification is only valid with plain water, not with:

(1) water previously used for purification (R: unless it has now been added together until it amounts to *216 liters* (Ar. qullatayn) or more);

(2) water changed (R: *change* meaning (n: throughout the rulings below) in taste, color, or odor, so much that it is no longer termed *water*) through admixture (R: with something pure (tahir) (n: meaning not affected with filth) like flour or saffron, which could have been avoided);

(3) or *impure* water, meaning less than 216 liters of water into which filth (najasa, def: 2.3) has fallen. (R: Less than 216 liters becomes impure by mere contact with filth, whether the water changes or not, unless filth falls into it whose amount before it falls in is so slight that it is indiscernible by eyesight (meaning an average look, not a negligent glance nor yet a minute inspection). As for 216 liters (n: or more), it does not become impure by mere contact with filth, but only becomes so by changing (n: in taste, color, or smell) because of it, even when this change is only slight. If such change disappears by itself, such as through standing at length or by water being added to it, even if the added water is used or impure, then the water is again purifying.)

Types of Filth (Najasa)

2.3 *Filth* (najasa) means:

(1) blood;

(2) (R: pus);

(3) vomit;

(4) liquid intoxicants;

(5) anything that exits from the front or rear private parts other than sperm or female sexual fluid (n: the latter meaning that normally released in orgasm);

(6) any animate life that dies without being Islamically slaughtered other than aquatic life (n: excluding amphibians, which are filth if unslaughtered), locusts, or human beings;

(7) and dogs, swine, or their offspring.

A body part separated from a living being is considered (n: in respect to being filth or not) like the unslaughtered dead of that animal, except for the hair of those animals that Muslims may eat after slaughtering (n: i.e. such hair is pure).

2.4 Wine becomes pure if it turns to vinegar by itself. So do hides of unslaughtered dead animals if tanned. (R: *Tanning* means removing from a hide all excess blood, fat, hair, and so on, by using an acrid substance, even if impure.) The hides of dogs or swine cannot be made pure by tanning.

Purifying Articles from Filth

2.5 Whatever is affected by their saliva (R:—by traces of moisture from dogs or swine, whether saliva, urine, anything moist from them, or any of their dry parts that have become moist) can only be purified by being washed seven times, one of which must be with earth (R: though if something dry such as the animal's breath or hair touches one's person, it need only be brushed away).

Articles affected with any other form of filth can be purified by washing it completely away with water just once, though three times is better.

Something affected with the urine of a male infant that has eaten nothing besides its mother's milk can be purified by sprinkling water over most of the spot.

The dead of animals without flowing blood (R: such as flies and the like) are excusable for purposes of ritual purity, as is a little pus or blood (n: on one's person, when praying, for example).

2.6 It is permissible to use any vessels or containers besides those made with gold or silver.

If there is confusion between a pure vessel and one affected with filth, one should take care to make sure to distinguish the one from the other.

The Toothstick (Siwak)

2.7 Using a toothstick (siwak) (R: a twig or the like on the teeth and around them, to remove an unpleasant change in the breath or similar, together with the intention of performing the sunna) is recommended except after noon for someone who is fasting. It is especially recommended for rising from sleep, performing the prayer, and any change in breath.

The Four Causes of Minor Ritual Impurity (Hadath)

2.8 Ablution (wudu) is necessitated by (n: i.e. is nullified by, and must be renewed after, any of the following four things, termed causes of *minor ritual impurity* (hadath), if one wants to perform something that may only be done with ablution, such as the prayer (salat), touching the Koran, and so forth):

(1) anything that exits from the front or rear private parts;

(2) loss of intellect (R: meaning the loss of the ability to distinguish, whether through insanity, unconsciousness, sleep, or other. *Loss of intellect* excludes drowsing and daydreaming, which do not nullify ablution. Among the signs of *drowsing* is that one can hear the words of those present, even if uncomprehendingly)—unless one falls asleep while firmly seated (R: on the ground or other surface firm enough to prevent a person's breaking wind while seated on it asleep);

(3) contact between the two skins of a man and a woman (R: husband and wife, for example) when they are not

each other's unmarriageable kin (mahram) and there is no barrier (n: such as a layer of cloth) between them;

(4) and touching human private parts with the palm or inner surfaces of the fingers (R: i.e. those surfaces that touch when the hands are put together, palm to palm.

Ablution is not nullified by vomiting, letting blood, nosebleed, laughing during the prayer, eating camel meat, or other things not discussed above).

2.9 (R: When certain that minor ritual impurity (hadath) has occurred, but uncertain whether one subsequently lifted it with ablution, then one is in a state of minor ritual impurity (because in Sacred Law, a state whose existence one is certain about does not cease through a state whose existence one is uncertain about).

When certain that one had ablution, but uncertain that it was subsequently nullified, then one still has ablution.)

Ablution (Wudu)

2.10 The obligatory *integrals* (Ar. *rukn,* pl. *arkan,* one of the legally essential elements found within an action that compose it) of ablution are:

(a) to have the intention (R: when one starts to wash the face);

(b) to wash the face (R: meaning from the point where the hairline usually begins to the chin in height, and from ear to ear in width);

(c) to wash the arms up to and including the elbows (R: if dirt under the nails prevents the water of ablution (or the purificatory bath (ghusl, def: 2.19)) from reaching the skin beneath, then the ablution (or bath) is not valid. The same is true of waterproof glue, paint, nail polish, and so forth on the nails or skin: if it prevents water from reaching *any part* of the nails or skin, no matter how small, one's ablution or purificatory bath is not valid);

(d) to wipe some of the head (n: scalp) with wet hands;

(e) to wash the feet up to and including the anklebones;

(f) and to do these things in the order mentioned.

2.11 The sunnas of ablution (wudu) are:

(1) to begin with the *Basmala* (n: the words *Bismi Llāhi r-Raḥmāni r-Raḥīm* (10.7) ("In the name of Allah, Most Merciful and Compassionate"));

(2) to wash one's hands (R: three times) before dipping them into the water container;

(3) to rinse out the mouth and nose (R: three times. One takes in a mouthful from a handful of water and snuffs up some of the rest of the handful into the nostrils (swishing the water around the mouth, and expelling the water of the mouth and the nose simultaneously), then again rinses the mouth and then the nostrils from a second handful of water, followed by rinsing the mouth and then the nostrils from a third handful of water);

(4) to cover the entire scalp area when wiping the head with wet hands (n: at (d) above);

(5) to wipe the ears (R: inside and out with new water three times, and then the ear canals with one's little fingers with more new water three times);

(6) to interlace the fingers (n: when washing one's hands to ensure that water reaches between them) and saturate between the toes (R: using the little finger of the left hand. One begins with the little toe of the right foot, coming up through the toes from beneath, and finishes with the little toe of the left);

(7) to saturate one's beard, if thick, by combing it from beneath with wet fingers;

(8) to begin with the right (R: when washing arms and legs, but not the hands, cheeks, and ears, which are washed right and left simultaneously);

(9) to wash (n: or wipe, if called for) each part three times (R: the obligatory minimum is once, though the sunna is to perform them each three times);

(10) to wash the parts of the body successively and without pausing between them (R: though if one pauses between them, even for a long time, one's ablution is still valid without renewing the intention);

Wiping Footgear

2.12 Wiping one's footgear (khuff) with wet hands (R: a dispensation that can take the place of the fifth ablution integral of washing the feet) is permissible to a nontraveller for 24 hours and to a traveller for 72 hours (the beginning of the period being reckoned from the time of the first minor ritual impurity (hadath, def: 2.8) that occurs after having put them on while in a state of ablution (wudu)), provided:

(a) that one have full ablution when one first puts them on;

(b) (R: that they be free of filth (najasa, def: 2.3));

(c) that they be durable enough to keep walking around upon (R: as travellers do in attending to their needs when encamping, departing, etc.);

(d) that they cover the whole foot up to and including the anklebones (R: provided none of the foot shows. One may not wipe footgear if wearing just one, washing the other foot. Nor if any of the foot shows through a hole in them);

(e) (R: and that they prevent water, if dripped on them drop by drop, from directly reaching the foot. If water reaches the foot through the holes of a seam's stitches, it does not affect the validity of wiping them, though if water can reach the foot through any other place, it violates this condition).

(R: The footgear Muslims generally use for this are ankle-high leather socks that zip up and are worn inside the shoes) (n: though they may be made of anything that fulfills the conditions) (R: including thick, heavy, wool socks that prevent water from reaching the foot (n: *directly,* i.e. by shedding the first few drops, as heavy wool does), but not modern dress socks (n: due to non-(c) and (e) above).)

2.13 (R: It is sunna to wipe the footgear on the top, bottom, and heel in lines, as if combing something with the fingers, without covering every part of them or wiping them more than once.

One puts the left hand under the heel and the right hand on top of the foot at the toes, drawing the right hand back towards the shin while drawing the left along the bottom of the foot in the opposite direction towards the toes.

It is sufficient as *wiping the footgear* to wipe any part of their upper surface with wet hands, from the top of the foot up to the level of the anklebones. It is not sufficient to only wipe some of the bottom, heel, side of the foot, or some of the footgear's inner surface that faces the skin.)

2.14 The validity of wiping the footgear is nullified by:

(1) taking them off;

(2) the permissible period for wiping them expiring;

(3) or the occurrence of a state of major ritual impurity (janaba, def: 2.17).

(R: When some part of the foot shows because of taking them off, or through a hole, or at the end of their permissible period, one removes the footgear to perform ablution (wudu), or, if one has ablution at the time, to wash the feet, before putting them on again and starting a new period of permissibility.

If a state of major ritual impurity (janaba) occurs during the permissible period for wiping footgear, one must take them off for the purificatory bath (ghusl, def: 2.19).)

Going to the Lavatory

2.15 It is obligatory to clean oneself of every impure substance (R: coming from one's front or rear, though not from gas). It is sunna to do so with a stone, followed by water. Water alone suffices, or three stones if these entirely remove the filth from the place, provided they fulfill the conditions (n: mentioned next) that permit one not to use water. (R: Anything (n: such as tissue paper) can take the place of stones that is a solid, pure, removes the filth, and is not something that deserves respect or is worthy of veneration, nor something that is edible, these being five conditions for the validity of using stones or something else to clean oneself of filth without having to follow it by washing with water. "Cleaning oneself" with a dry substance means to remove the filth so that nothing remains but a trace that could not be removed unless one were to use water, and when this has been done, any remaining effects of filth that could have only been removed with water are excusable. But it is obligatory to wash oneself with water if:

(1) one has washed away the filth with a liquid other than water, or with something impure;

(2) one has become soiled with filth from a separate source;

(3) one's waste has moved from where it exited (reaching another part of one's person) or has dried;

(4) or if feces has spread beyond the inner buttocks (meaning that which is enfolded when standing), or urine moved beyond the head of the penis, though if they do not pass beyond them, stones suffice.)

2.16 (R: It is offensive to use the right hand to clean oneself of filth.)

It is unlawful to urinate (R: or defecate) with front or rear towards the direction of prayer (qibla) when outdoors (R: and there is no barrier to screen one, though this is permissible, when outdoors or in, within a meter and a half of a barrier at least 32 cm. high, or in a hole that deep. When one is not this close to such a barrier, it is not permissible except in a lavatory, where, if the walls are farther from one than the maximal distance or are shorter than the minimal height, relieving oneself with front or rear towards the direction of prayer is permissible, though offensive.)

It is offensive to relieve oneself into still water, under fruit trees, on paths, in the shade (n: i.e. where people gather to talk), into holes, (n: or while standing, (R: which is offensive unless there is an excuse, such as when standing is less likely to spatter urine on one's clothes than sitting, or when sitting is a hardship).)

It is offensive to speak when relieving oneself.

The Causes of Major Ritual Impurity (Janaba)

2.17 The purificatory bath (ghusl, def: 2.19) is necessitated by (n: i.e. nullified by, and must be renewed after any of the following, the first two of which are termed *causes of major ritual impurity* (janaba). All that is forbidden in a state of major ritual impurity (def: 2.30) is forbidden after any of the following actions, until one performs the purificatory bath):

(1) the head of the penis entering the vagina;

(2) the exit of sperm from a male; or female sexual fluid (meaning that which comes from orgasm) from a female;

(3) death;

(4) the end of a woman's menstrual period;

(5) the end her postnatal bleeding;

(6) or after giving birth (R: if a child is born in a dry birth) (n: i.e. in the rare event of a birth without postnatal bleeding, for otherwise she waits till after her bleeding ceases).

2.18 (R: Male sperm and female sexual fluid are recognized by the fact that they:

(1) come in spurts (by contractions);

(2) with sexual gratification;

(3) and when moist, smell like bread dough, and when dry, like egg-white.

When a substance from the genital orifice has any *one* of the above characteristics, then it is sperm or sexual fluid and makes the purificatory bath obligatory. When not even one of the above characteristics is present, it is not sperm or sexual fluid. Being white or thick is not necessary for it to be considered male sperm, and being yellow or thin is not necessary for it to be considered female sexual fluid.

The purificatory bath is not obligatory when there is an unlustful discharge of thin, sticky, white fluid (madhy) caused by amorous play or kissing; or when there is a discharge of the thick, cloudy, white fluid (wady) that exits after urinating or carrying something heavy.)

The Purificatory Bath (Ghusl)

2.19 The purificatory bath (ghusl) has two obligatory features:

(a) that one intend (R: the purificatory bath, or to lift a state of major ritual impurity (janaba) or menstruation, or to be permitted to perform the prayer);

(b) and that one wash all of the skin (dis: 2.10(c)) and hair (R: to the roots of the hair, under nails, and the outwardly visible portion of the ear canals).

Its sunnas are: to (n: first) perform ablution (wudu); to rub the body while bathing; and to wash the body parts consecutively and without interruption.

(R: Whoever performs the bath one time with the intention to both lift a state of major ritual impurity and fulfill the sunna of the Friday prayer bath has performed both, though if he only intends one, his bath counts for that one but not the other.)

2.20 The purificatory bath is sunna:

(1) for attending the Friday prayer (jum'a) (R: the bath's time beginning at dawn);

(2) on the two 'Eids (n: *'Eid al-Fitr* at the end of Ramadan and *'Eid al-Adha* on 10 Dhul Hijja) (R: its time beginning from the middle of the night);

(3) on days when the sun or moon eclipse;

(4) before the drought prayer (istisqa');

(5) upon becoming a Muslim (n: though it is not merely sunna but rather *obligatory* if any of the things mentioned at 2.17 above have occurred before becoming Muslim);

(6) after recovering one's sanity, or regaining consciousness after having lost it;

(7) before entering the state of pilgrim sanctity (ihram, def: 6.2(a)), when entering Mecca, for standing at 'Arafa (6.2(b)), and for each day of stoning at Mina (6.4(b)) on the three days following 'Eid al-Adha;

(8) and after washing the dead (R: and it is sunna to perform ablution (wudu) after touching a corpse).

Dry Ablution (Tayammum)

2.21 (R: When unable to use water, dry ablution is a dispensation to perform the prayer or similar act without lifting one's minor or major impurity, by the use of earth for one's ablution.) The conditions for the legal validity of performing dry ablution (tayammum) are:

(a) that one lack water, or fear to use it (n: *fear* including both from thirst (R: one's own thirst, or that of companions and animals with one, even if in the future) and from illness (R: an ailment from which one fears that performing a normal ablution (wudu) or purificatory bath (ghusl) would cause: harm to life or limb, disability, becoming seriously ill, an increase in one's ailment, a delay in recovering from one's illness, considerable pain, or (a bad effect from the water such as) a radical change in one's skin color on a visible part of the body. One's own previous experience may be sufficient to establish the probability that one of these will occur if a full ablution or bath is performed. Or one may depend on a physician whose information concerning it is acceptable, meaning one with skill in medicine whose word can be believed, even if he is not a Muslim));

(b) that dry ablution take place after the beginning of the prayer's time (R: if it is for an obligatory prayer or a nonobligatory one that has a particular time);

(c) that if lacking water, one search for some before performing dry ablution (R: When one is sure there is none, one performs dry ablution without searching for it);

(d) and that one use earth (R: plain, purifying earth that contains dust, even the dust contained in sand, though not pure sand devoid of dust).

2.22 The integrals of dry ablution are:

(a) that one make the intention (R: when one first strikes the earth, and it must continue until one wipes part of the face) for authorization (R: to perform the obligation of the prayer or that which requires dry ablution);

(b) (R: that the dry ablution be performed by striking the earth twice, once for wiping the face, and a second time for wiping the arms);

(c) that one's hands convey the earth (R: up to the face and arms, after having shaken the excess dust from one's hands);

(d and e) to wipe the face (R: not missing under the nose) and hands and arms up to and including the elbows;

(f) and to do the above in the order mentioned.

2.23 The sunnas of dry ablution are:

(1) to begin with the *Basmala* (n: the words *Bismi Llāhi r-Raḥmāni r-Raḥīm* ("In the name of Allah, Most Merciful and Compassionate"));

(2) to wipe the right arm before the left;

(3) to wipe the arms immediately after (n: striking the earth after wiping) the face, without pause between them;

(4) (R: and for wiping the arms, holding the palms up, to place the left hand crosswise under the right with the left hand's fingers touching the backs of the fingers of the right hand, sliding the left hand up to the right wrist. Then, curling the fingers around the side of the right wrist, one slides the left hand to the right elbow, then turns the left palm so it rests on the top of the right forearm with its thumb pointed away from one before sliding it back down to the wrist, where one wipes the back of the right thumb with the inside of the left thumb. One then wipes the left arm in the same manner, followed by interlacing the fingers, rubbing the palms together, and then dusting the hands off lightly).

2.24 Dry ablution is nullified by:

(1) the occurrence of ritual impurity (n: whether minor (def: 2.8) or major (2.17));

(2) or the appearance of water, when one is not in prayer (R: This belief (n: that one can now obtain water) also nullifies dry ablution when it occurs during one's prayer if the prayer is one which must be later made up, like that of someone at home who performs dry ablution for lack of water (because if one performs dry ablution in a place where water is generally available during the whole year, it is obligatory to make up one's prayer, in view of the fact that the dry ablution has been performed for a rare excuse. The rule is that whoever performs the prayer without full ritual purity because of a rare excuse is obliged to make up his prayer, as when the water of a city or village is cut off for a brief period of time during which those praying perform dry ablution, while if one has performed it in a place where water is seldom available during the year, it is not obligatory to make up one's prayer, as when one performs dry ablution in the

desert). But if not of those prayers that must be made up later, such as that of a desert traveller who has performed dry ablution, then the belief that one can now obtain water, when it occurs during prayer, does not nullify one's dry ablution, and one finishes the prayer, which is adequate, though it is recommended to interrupt it in order to begin again after one has performed ablution.)

2.25 One must perform one dry ablution for each prescribed prayer (R: though one may perform any number of nonobligatory prayers or funeral prayers with it).

Dry Ablution (Tayammum) for Injuries

2.26 If one has a bandage or cast (n: on a part of the body normally washed in ablution, a dressing that one could not remove without causing oneself harm), one wipes it with water (R: when one comes to it in the ablution sequence) in addition to performing a complete dry ablution (R: at that point).

One need not later make up prescribed prayers performed with such an ablution, provided that one had ablution when the bandage or cast was first applied (n: and provided it is not on the face or arms, as discussed next) (R: when someone with such a bandage on the members of dry ablution (the face or arms) recovers and has his cast or dressing removed, he is obliged to make up (repray) all the prayers he performed with such an ablution.

The Hanafi school requires someone with an injury who wants to pray to make a complete ablution (or bath (ghusl), if needed). But if this would entail harm (n: one of the things mentioned above at 2.21(a)), then when he comes to the injury in the ablution sequence, he is merely required to wipe it with wet hands so as to cover more than half of the injury. If this would also entail harm, or if he has a bandage that cannot be removed without harm, or he cannot reapply the dressing by himself and has no one to help him to do so, then he simply wipes more than half the bandage when he comes to it in his ablution. He may pray with such an ablution and need not repeat the prayer later (*al-Hadiyya al-'Alā'iyya* (9.1), 43–44). It is not necessary that he be free of minor or even major impurity (janaba) at the time the dressing is applied (*al-Lubāb fī sharḥ al-Kitāb* (9.16), 1.41).

There is strong evidence for performing dry ablution in place of washing such an injury. To add it at the proper point of the ablution sequence as a precautionary measure would not interfere with the validity of following the Hanafi position just discussed).

Menstruation and Postnatal Bleeding

2.27 Menstruation may begin after the age of nine. The minimal menstrual period is a day and a night. The maximum is 15 days. Postnatal bleeding (nifas) lasts at least a moment, and at most 60 days. If it lasts longer than the maximum, it is considered to be chronic vaginal discharge (dis: 2.28). The minimal interval of purity between two menstruations is 15 days. There is no maximal limit to the number of days between menstruations.

(R: Whenever a woman who is old enough notices her bleeding, even if pregnant, she must avoid what a woman in her period avoids (def: 2.30 (end)). If it ceases in less than 24 hours (lit. "the minimum"), then it is not considered menstruation, and the woman must make up the prayers she has omitted during it. If it ceases at 24 hours, within 15 days, or between the two, then it is menstruation. If it exceeds 15 days, then she is a woman with chronic vaginal discharge (dis: 2.28).

Yellow or dusky colored discharge is considered menstrual flow.

If a woman has times of intermittent bleeding and cessation during an interval of 15 days or less, and the times of bleeding collectively amount to at least 24 hours, then the entire interval, bleeding and nonbleeding, is considered menstruation.)

Chronic Annulment of Ablution

2.28 (R: A woman with chronic vaginal discharge preparing to pray should wash her private parts, apply something absorbent to them and a dressing, and then perform ablution. She may not delay commencing her prayer after this except for reasons of preparing to pray such as clothing her nakedness, awaiting the call to prayer (adhan), or for a group to gather for the prayer. If she delays for other reasons, she must repeat the purification.

She is obliged to wash her private parts, apply a dressing, and perform ablution before each obligatory prayer, though she is entitled, like those mentioned below, to perform as many nonobligatory prayers as she wishes, carry and read the Koran, and so on, until the next prayer's time comes or until her ablution is broken for a different reason, when she must renew the above measures and her ablution.)

2.29 (R: People unable to hold back intermittent drops of urine coming from them must take the same measures that a woman with chronic vaginal discharge does. And likewise for anyone in a state of chronic annulment of ablution, such as continually breaking wind, excrement, or *madhy* (def: 2.18(end)), though washing and applying an absorbent dressing are only obligatory when filth exits.

If a person knows that drops of urine will not stop until the time for the next prayer comes, he takes the above measures and performs the prayer at the first of its time.)

Actions Unlawful Without Ritual Purity

2.30 The following are unlawful for someone in a state of minor ritual impurity (hadath, def: 2.8):

(1) to perform the prayer;

(2) (R: to prostrate when reciting the Koran at verses in which it is sunna to do so;

(3) to prostrate out of thanks);

(4) to circumambulate the Kaaba;

(5) and to touch or carry a Koran.

The preceding are also unlawful for someone in a state of major ritual impurity (janaba, def: 2.17), as are:

(6) to recite the Koran;

(7) and to remain in a mosque.

During menstruation and postnatal bleeding, all of the above are unlawful, as well as:

(8) to take sexual enjoyment from what is between the navel and knees, until the purificatory bath (ghusl, def: 2.19) is performed;

(9) or to fast, until menstruation or postnatal bleeding ceases. (R: The obligatory fast-days she misses must be made up later, though not missed prayers.)

3

THE PRAYER (SALAT)

الصلاة

CONTENTS:

Times of Prescribed Prayers

3.1 The prescribed prayers are five, which are obligatory for every Muslim who has reached the age of puberty and is sane:

(1) The time for the *noon prayer* (dhuhr) begins after the sun has reached its zenith, and ends when an object's shadow (R: minus the length of its shadow at the time of the sun's zenith) equals the object's height.

(2) The time for the *midafternoon prayer* ('asr) begins at the end of the noon prayer's time. The preferred time for its performance ends when an object's shadow (R: minus the length of its shadow at the time of the sun's zenith) is twice as long as the object's height, though the permissible time for it extends until the sun sets.

(3) The time for the *sunset prayer* (maghrib) begins when

the sun has completely set, and ends when the red disappears from the sky.

(4) The time for the *nightfall prayer* ('isha) begins at the end of the sunset prayer's time. The preferred time for its performance ends when a third of the night has passed, though its permissible time extends until dawn.

(5) And the time for the *dawn prayer* (subh) begins at true dawn (R: *true dawn* being when the sky around the horizon begins to grow light. Before this, a dim light sometimes appears overhead for some minutes, followed by darkness, and is termed the deceptive dawn (al-fajr al-kadhib)). The preferred time for its performance ends when the day grows light outside, though its permissible time extends until sunrise.

(R: It is best to pray every prayer at the first of its time, taking the necessary steps at its outset, such as purification, clothing one's nakedness, giving the call to prayer (adhan) and call to commence (iqama), and then praying.

If less that one *rak'a* (n: a full cycle of the prayer's words and actions) of the prayer occurs within the proper time (meaning that one does not lift one's head from the second prostration of the rak'a before the time ends, and the remainder takes place after it) then the whole prayer is considered a makeup. If one rak'a or more takes place within the prayer's time and the remainder is after it, then the prayer is considered a current performance, though it is unlawful to intentionally delay the prayer until part of it occurs after the time has finished.)

(n: Prayer times vary a little each day with the season and the year, and from one town to another through the effects of latitude and longitude. One can keep oneself informed of the changes by obtaining the whole year's times in a printed calendar from one's local Muslim association or mosque, or (particularly useful for travellers) by using any of several pocket computers now available that calculate them, such as the Prayer Minder, which is based on precise astronomical data, programmed for fifty years, and when given various cities' geographical coordinates supplied in the accompanying booklet, provides the prayer times of most major cities in the world.)

(R: If one's location does not have one or more of the prayer times, such as nightfall (because of twilight all night), sunrise, etc., due to the extreme northerly latitude, then one should pray at the same time as the closest city that has the true times. For each degree of longitude that this closest city lies to the east of one's location, the prayer time of the city will arrive earlier than at one's own position by four minutes, and one may wish to compensate for this error factor by the appropriate calculations, i.e. not praying simultaneously with that city's times, but rather after its time by four minutes for each degree of longitude it lies to the east, or before its time by four minutes for each degree of longitude it lies to the west, in addition to observing time zone differences, if it is in a different one.

For both the dawn prayer (subh) and the dawn that marks the beginning of fast-days of Ramadan, if there is sunset and sunrise at one's location but not true dawn because of the persistence of twilight all night, one copies the nearest city that has the true times in terms of the amount of time by which dawn in that city precedes sunrise there. Thus if dawn in this nearest city precedes sunrise by 90 minutes, one's own "dawn" occurs 90 minutes before the sunrise in one's own city. And similarly for the amount of time by which nightfall ('isha) follows the sunset prayer (maghrib).

Finally, if one finds one has been consistently mistaken about the time of a particular prayer, and performed it day after day in other than its time, one has only one prayer to make up (that of the last day), as each day is considered the makeup of the day before it.)

Making Up Missed Prayers

3.2 (R: When enough of a prayer's time has elapsed to have performed the prayer during it, and someone who has not yet prayed loses their reason or their menstrual period begins, they are obligated to make up that missed prayer as soon as they are able.

Whenever a prescribed prayer is missed for a valid reason (n: such as being asleep, or forgetting it), it is recommended to make it up immediately. If missed without a valid reason, it is obligatory to make it up immediately.)

Times When the Prayer Is Forbidden

3.3 (R: The rules below apply to prayers that are wholly supererogatory, i.e. which are not performed for any particular occasion or reason, and apply to prayers performed for a reason that will occur after the prayer, such as the two sunna rak'as before entering the state of pilgrim sanctity (ihram, def: 6.2(a)).)

One may not perform prayers that have no particular occasion or reason (R: i.e. the prayer is unlawful and invalid):

(1) from after the dawn prayer (subh) until the sun is well up (R: meaning when a distance equal to the sun's diameter appears between the sun and the horizon);

(2) from the time of the sun's zenith until it moves on;

(3) from after the midafternoon prayer ('asr) until sunset, and from when the afternoon sun yellows until sunset;

(R: It is permissible at the above times to offer nonobligatory prayers that are performed for a particular reason, such as the funeral prayer, greeting the mosque, or the two rak'as that are sunna after ablution (wudu); and is also permissible to make up missed prayers; though one may not perform the two rak'as that are sunna before entering the state of pilgrim sanctity (ihram, def: 6.2(a)).

It is not offensive to pray within the Meccan Sacred Precinct (Haram) at any time. Nor is it offensive to pray when the sun is at its zenith on Fridays, whether in the Sacred Precinct or elsewhere.)

Sunna Prayers

3.4 It is sunna to perform the prayer: on the Two 'Eids (n: *'Eid al-Fitr* at the end of Ramadan, and *'Eid al-Adha* on 10 Dhul Hijja), when the sun or moon eclipse, and to ask for rain when there is a drought.

3.5 It is (n: of the confirmed) sunna (R: *confirmed* (mu'akkada) meaning those which the Prophet (Allah bless him and give him peace) did not omit whether travelling or at home) to perform:

(1) two rak'as before the dawn prayer (subh);

(2) two before and after the noon prayer (dhuhr);

(3) two after the sunset prayer (maghrib);

(4) two after the nightfall prayer ('isha);

(5) and *witr* (R: the minimal performance for *witr* is one rak'a, even if one omits the sunnas after the nightfall prayer ('isha). The optimal way is to perform eleven rak'as, and one should finish with Salams after every pair. The least considered optimal is three rak'as, and one separates them by finishing two times with Salams (i.e. by finishing two rak'as with Salams and the performing the final rak'a). It is recommended to recite al-A'la (Koran 87) in the first rak'a, al-Kafirun (Koran 109) in the second, and al-Ikhlas, al-Falaq, and al-Nas (Koran 112, 113, and 114) in the third. The best time for *witr* is just after the sunna rak'as that follow the nightfall prayer, unless one intends to offer the *night vigil prayer* (tahajjud; to rise at night after having slept, to pray some nonobligatory rak'as), in which case it is best to pray *witr* after the night vigil prayer).

It is also recommended to perform:

(6) two additional rak'as before the noon prayer and after it (n: making four before and four after);

(7) four rak'as before the midafternoon prayer;

(8) the midmorning prayer (duha) (R: which minimally consists of two rak'as, is optimally eight rak'as, and maximally twelve. One finishes each pair of rak'as with Salams);

(9) *tarawih* (R: which is twenty rak'as of group prayer on each night of Ramadan (i.e. as well as being sunna to pray *tarawih* alone, it is also sunna to pray it in a group). One finishes each pair of rak'as with Salams);

(10) and the night vigil prayer (tahajjud) (R: Supererogatory prayer at night is a confirmed sunna, even if one can only do a little. It is recommended to begin one's night vigil prayers with two brief rak'as, to have intended the night vigil prayer before going to sleep, and not to make a practice of more prayer than one can regularly perform without harm to oneself).

Performing the Prayer

3.6 (n:) The translator has added the following description (3.7–3.10) of the prayer as a framework in which to understand Nawawi's summary below at 3.11 of the elements that compose it. Words with specific technical senses have been given with cross-reference numbers to the paragraphs that describe them.

Before the Prayer

3.7 The preconditions for validly performing the prayer are:

(a) That if one is in a state of minor ritual impurity (hadath, def: 2.8), one perform ablution (wudu, 2.10); and if in a state of major ritual impurity (janaba, 2.17), or after menstruation or postnatal bleeding, one perform the purificatory bath (ghusl, 2.19). If one was previously in a state of purity, and uncertain as to whether something has happened to nullify it, then one is still considered to be in a state of purity.

(b) That one remove all filth (najasa, 2.3, 2.15) from one's body, clothes, and place of prayer, the latter meaning the area on the ground that is in actual contact with one's person when performing it. If one is not absolutely sure that something is affected with filth (as when it is merely likely), then it is considered not to be, as the initial presumption for all things is purity.

(c) That one clothe one's nakedness. Men's clothing must at least cover the entire surface of the skin from the knees up to and including the navel. Women's clothing must at least cover the entire body, excepting the face and hands alone. If anything else shows during the prayer, such as through a hole in the clothing, or the skin of a man's back from between his shirt and pants while prostrating, or a strand of a woman's hair from under her headcover, or part of her feet—the prayer must be repeated, unless one covered the exposed part immediately.

(d) That one know or believe a prayer's time (def: 3.1) has come.

(e) That one face the direction of the Kaaba in Mecca. To establish the direction of prayer in cities far from Mecca, one may use a world globe and a piece of string, since in North America and other regions, using a flat world map will yield the wrong direction because of the curvature of the earth. One puts the end of the string on the position of Mecca on the globe, the other end on one's own city, and pulls the string taut, observing the bearing of the string and drawing a line in the same direction on a local map, which can be oriented with a compass and used to indicate the proper direction to pray.

Facing the direction of prayer is obligatory in all prescribed prayers. In nonobligatory prayers, if one is riding and is able to face the direction of prayer, to stand, bow, and prostrate, one must. If not able, one is only required to face the direction of prayer during the first Allahu Akbar of the prayer, if not difficult, though if difficult, one is not obliged to face the direction of prayer at any point of the prayer's performance, and one merely nods in the direction of travel instead of bowing and prostrating. One's nod for prostration must be deeper than the nod for bowing.

If unable to face the direction of prayer, stand, and so on for an obligatory prayer, one takes these same measures, and later makes up the prayer when able to properly perform it.

How to Perform the Prayer

3.8 The "works of the heart" are the soul of the prayer, without which its outward form would be but empty words and motions. One's sole aim should be Allah Himself, offering the worship that is due to Him out of love and thanks. Islamic scholars such as Imam al-Ghazali tell us that the rewards for spiritual works mentioned in Koran and hadith are for acts whose basis is such sincerity of intention, not when motivated by a sort of commercial avidness for spiritual gain. Allah Most High says:

"Nor were they commanded, save to make their religion sincerely for Him" (Koran 98:5),

and

"So whoever longs to meet his Lord, let him work righteousness, and associate none with his Lord's worship" (Koran 18:110).

The prayer should also be performed with the humility and presence of mind befitting our relation to the nature of the Divine, as Allah has commanded us upon the tongue of his Prophet (Allah bless him and give him peace), who said,

"Pray as you have seen me pray" [Bukhari, Muslim].

The prayer is described next, first in summary, then in detail.

3.9 The actions of the prayer are:

—Standing facing the direction of prayer, raising the hands, and saying *Allāhu akbar* (10.8) ("Allah is greatest").

—Folding the hands over the breast, reciting the *Fatiha* (first sura of the Koran) and then another sura or some other verses of the Koran, chosen at will.

—Bowing and placing the hands on the knees, one's back horizontal.

—Straightening back up to a standing position, raising the hands to shoulder height and then lowering them.

—Prostrating by kneeling, then bowing forward, placing the flat palms of the hands on the ground below the shoulders, and then forehead and nose on the ground.

—Sitting back.

—Prostrating a second time.

This constitutes a full *rak'a* or cycle of the prayer's actions, which is repeated varying numbers of times according to which prayer is being performed: two for dawn prayer (subh), four for noon (dhuhr), four for midafternoon ('asr), three for sunset (maghrib), and four for nightfall ('isha). At the end of the second rak'a, after prostrating the second time, one sits back and recites the Testification of Faith (Tashahhud), as also at the end of the last rak'a of prayers with more than two rak'as, when instead of rising for a new rak'a, one turns the head to the right and says *al-Salāmu 'alaykum* (10.9) ("Peace be upon you") to finish the prayer, and then turns to the left and says it again. The description below explains these steps in greater detail.

3.10 The steps of the prayer are performed as follows:

(1) One stands facing the direction of prayer, lifting the open hands to shoulder level, palms facing forward. One opens the prayer by saying *Allāhu akbar* (10.10) ("Allah is greatest"), intending performance of the particular obligatory prayer one is offering (e.g. "the dawn obligatory prayer").

The minimal audibility for pronouncing the opening Allahu Akbar, reciting the Koran, and all invocations is that one can hear them oneself under normal conditions.

It is obligatory to stand in all prescribed prayers for anyone who is able, though if one is unable to stand, or performing a nonobligatory prayer, one may sit.

(2) After the opening Allahu Akbar, one places the hands between the chest and navel, grasping the left wrist with the right hand, and fixing one's gaze on the place where one's forehead will prostrate. It is offensive to close one's eyes while praying unless it is more conducive to awe and humility towards Allah.

(3) Then, in the first rak'a only, one is recommended to recite (dis: 1.12) the Opening Supplication (Istiftah), which is: *Wajjahtu wajhī li lladhī faṭara s-samāwāti wa l-arḍa ḥanīfan Musliman wa mā anā mina l-mushrikīn; inna ṣalātī wa nusukī wa maḥyāya wa mamātī li Llāhi Rabbi l-'Ālamīna lā sharīka lah, wa bi dhālika umirtu wa anā mina l-Muslimīn* (10.11) ("I turn my face to Him who created the heavens and earth, a pure monotheist, in submission, and am not of those who associate others with Him. My prayer, worship, life, and death are for Allah, Lord of the Worlds, who has no partner. Thus I have been commanded, and I am of those who submit").

(4) Then, in every rak'a, one is recommended to recite the Ta'awwudh, *A'ūdhu bi Llāhi mina sh-shayṭāni r-rajīm* (10.12) ("I take refuge in Allah from the accursed devil").

(5) Then, in every rak'a, whether praying alone or with others, it is obligatory to recite the Fatiha (the opening sura of the Koran), which is: *Bismi Llāhi r-Raḥmāni r-Raḥīm. al-Ḥamdu li Llāhi Rabbi l-'Ālamīn. al-Raḥmāni r-Raḥīm, Māliki Yawmi d-Dīn. Iyyāka na'budu wa iyyāka nasta'īn. Ihdina ṣ-ṣirāṭa l-mustaqīm. Ṣirāṭa lladhīna an'amta 'alayhim ghayri l-maghḍūbi 'alayhim wa la ḍ-ḍāllīn* (10.13) ("In the name of Allah, Most Merciful and Compassionate. All praise be to Allah, Lord of the Worlds, Most Merciful and Compassionate, Lord of the Day of Reckoning. You alone we worship, in You alone we seek help. Guide us the straight way. The way of those You have blessed, not of those upon whom is wrath or those who are lost" (Koran

1:1–7)).

After the Fatiha, one says *Āmīn* (10.14) ("Answer our prayer").

(6) Then, in the first two rak'as only, if praying alone or leading others as imam in the prayer or praying behind an imam whose recitation is not audible to one, it is recommended to recite some of the Koran, which should at least be three verses, though it is superior to recite a whole sura, even if short. One may recite, for example, one of the three last suras of the Koran:

Al-Ikhlas (Koran 112): *Bismi Llāhi r-Raḥmāni r-Raḥīm. Qul huwa Llāhu Aḥad, Allāhu ṣ-Ṣamad. Lam yalid, wa lam yūlad, wa lam yakun lahu kufuwan aḥad* (10.15) (In the name of Allah, Most Merciful and Compassionate. Say: 'He is Allah, One. Allah, the Ultimate. He has not begotten, nor was He begotten, and no one is equal to Him'").

Al-Falaq (Koran 113): *Bismi Llāhi r-Raḥmāni r-Raḥīm. Qul a'ūdhu bi Rabbi l-Falaq, min sharri mā khalaq, wa min sharri ghāsiqin idhā waqab, wa min sharri n-naffāthāti fi l-'uqad, wa min sharri ḥāsidin idhā ḥasad* (10.16) ("In the name of Allah, Most Merciful and Compassionate. Say: 'I take refuge in the Lord of the Dawn, from the evil of what He has created, from the evil of the night when it comes, from the evil of the women who blow on knots, and from the evil of the envier when he envies.'")

Al-Nas (Koran 114): *Bismi Llāhi r-Raḥmāni r-Raḥīm. Qul a'ūdhu bi Rabbi n-Nās, Maliki n-Nās, Ilāhi n-Nās, min sharri l-waswāsi l-khannās, alladhī yuwaswisu fī ṣudūri n-nās, mina l-jinnati wa n-nās* (10.17) ("In the name of Allah, Most Merciful and Compassionate. Say: 'I take refuge in the Lord of men, King of men, God of men, from the evil of the slinking whisperer, who whispers in the breasts of men, of jinn and men.'")

The Fatiha and sura are only recited aloud, when praying alone or leading others as imam, in the dawn prayer (subh) and the first two rak'as of the sunset (maghrib) and nightfall ('isha) prayers; as well as in the Friday (jum'a), 'Eid, drought, lunar eclipse, and *tarawih* group prayers.

When following an imam, performing other nonobligatory prayers, or the noon (dhuhr) or midafternoon ('asr) prayers, the Fatiha and sura are recited to oneself. One omits the sura when the imam's is audible.

(7) Then one bows from the waist, obligatorily. The minimum is to bow as far as an average size person needs to when he wants to put his hands on his knees.

It is obligatory that one *repose* therein (as in all physical postures of the prayer), minimally meaning to remain motionless for a moment after having reached the position.

The optimal way is to raise one's hands and say *Allāhu akbar* so that one begins raising the hands as one starts saying it, and when the hands are at shoulder level, one bows.

Whenever one says *Allāhu akbar* during a movement from one prayer posture to another (as is recommended at every change of posture except straightening up from bowing), it is recommended to prolong the words until one reaches the next posture.

Then one puts the hands on the knees, fingers apart, back and neck extended, legs straight, and elbows out (though women keep them close); saying, *Subḥāna Rabbiya l-'Aḏḥīm* (10.18) ("My Lord Most Great is exalted above any limitation"), three times.

(8) Then one straightens back up, returning to standing as one was before bowing, and remaining motionless in the upright position for at least a moment.

It is optimal to raise the hands (lifting them from the knees as one starts straightening up, raising them to shoulder level) and the head together, saying *Sami'a Llāhu li man ḥamidah* (10.19) ("Allah hears him who praises Him"), and when one reaches the upright position, *Rabbanā laka l-ḥamd* (10.20) ("Our Lord, Yours is the praise"), and one may complete it: *mil'a s-samāwāti wa mil'a l-arḍi wa mil'a mā shi'ta min shay'in ba'd* (10.21) ("heavensful, earthful, and whatever-else-You-will-ful").

(9) Then one prostrates, putting the knees down first, then the hands, then the forehead on the place of prayer. It is obligatory that one remain motionless therein at least a moment, that the place bear the weight of the head, that one's rear be higher than the head, that one not place the head on something joined to one's person such as a sleeve or turban, and that part of each knee, the bottom of the toes of the feet, and the fingers of the hands be placed on the ground.

The forehead is the only part that must be uncovered in prostration. It is not obligatory that the nose touch the ground in prostration, but it is desirable.

The optimal way is to say *Allāhu akbar,* to put the knees down first, then hands, then the forehead and nose. One prostrates with the hands directly under the shoulders, elbows raised (it is offensive for the forearms or elbows to touch the ground), fingers together and extended toward the direction of prayer. Men keep about one span (ca. 23 centimeters) between their two knees and two feet, though a woman's knees are kept together, and men keep the stomach apart from the thighs and forearms from sides, though women keep them together. One says while prostrating, *Subḥāna Rabbiya l-A'lā* (10.22) ("My Lord Most High is exalted above all limitation") three times.

(10) Then one raises the head and sits back on the heels, remaining motionless therein for a moment before prostrating a second time.

The optimal way is to say *Allāhu akbar* as one sits up; to sit in *iftirash,* which is to sit back on the heel of one's right foot which is upright and resting on the bottom of its toes, while the left foot is on its side, toes pointed toward the right; to place one's two hands on the thighs near the knees, fingers extended and held together; and to say, *Allāhumma ghfir lī wa rḥamnī wa 'āfinī wa jburnī wa hdinī wa rzuqnī* (10.23) ("O Allah, forgive me, have mercy on me, pardon me, set me right, guide me, and sustain me").

Then one prostrates again just as before. The first rak'a is only completed when one has performed the second prostration, because each prostration is a separate integral, as is the moment of motionlessness in each.

(11) After this one raises the head, saying *Allāhu akbar* as one first raises it, drawing out the words until one is standing upright.

It is sunna, here and in each rak'a that is not followed by the Testification of Faith (Tashahhud), to briefly rest in the *iftirash* style of sitting before rising. Then one rises, helping oneself up with both hands, palms down, and prolonging the Allahu Akbar until standing.

(12) Then one performs the second rak'a of the prayer just like the first, except for the initial intention, the opening Allahu Akbar, and Opening Supplication (Istiftah), which are omitted.

(13) If one's prayer exceeds two rak'as, one sits in *iftirash* after the first two rak'as and recites the Testification of Faith (Tashahhud, (15) below) and the Blessings on the Prophet (Allah bless him and give him peace), though not upon his family (which is done only in the final Testification of Faith at the end of the prayer).

Then one rises, saying *Allāhu akbar* and leaning on one's hands as before (at the end of (11) above). When standing, one lifts the hands to shoulder level (which one does here, but not after rising from the first or third rak'a), and then goes on to perform the remainder of the prayer as one did the second rak'a, except that one recites the Fatiha to oneself and does not recite a sura after it.

(14) One sits back after the second prostration of the last rak'a of the prayer for the Testification of Faith in the *tawarruk* style of sitting, with one's left posterior on the ground and left foot on its outer side, emerging from under the right, which is vertical.

However one sits here, in the final Testification of Faith

(Tashahhud), and in the previous one, as well as between the two prostrations and before risings, is permissible, though *iftirash* and *tawarruk* are sunna.

In the two Testifications of Faith, one's left hand rests on the left thigh near the knee, its fingers extended and held together. The right hand is similarly placed, but is held closed with its thumb touching the side of the index finger, which alone is left extended. One lifts the index finger and points with it when one says the words *illa Llāh.* (One does not move it while it is thus raised, following the sunna from a hadith related by Abu Dawud. It is offensive to move it here, though some hold that it is recommended, the evidence for which is also from the sunna, in a hadith related by Bayhaqi, who states that both hadiths are rigorously authenticated (sahih). Bayhaqi says that the meaning of *moving it* in the latter hadith is simply *raising* it, so there is no actual contradiction.)

(15) The Testification of Faith (Tashahhud) is to say: *At-taḥiyyātu l-mubārakātu ṣ-ṣalawātu ṭ-ṭayyibātu li Llāh, as-salāmu 'alayka ayyuha n-Nabiyyu wa raḥmatu Llāhi wa barakātuh, as-salāmu 'alayna wa 'alā 'ibādi Llāhi ṣ-ṣāliḥīn, ash-hadu an lā ilāha illa Llāh, wa ash-hadu anna Muḥammadan rasūlu Llāh* (10.24) ("Greetings, blessing, and the best of prayers to Allah. Peace be upon you, O Prophet, and the mercy of Allah and His blessings. Peace be upon us and upon Allah's righteous slaves. I testify there is no god except Allah, and that Muhammad is the Messenger of Allah").

(16) One then says the Blessings on the Prophet (Allah bless him and give him peace).

If in the first Testification of Faith of the prayer (at the end of the second rak'a of prayers that have more than two rak'as) one says, *Allāhumma ṣalli 'alā Sayyidinā Muḥammad* (10.25) ("O Allah, bless our liegelord Muhammad").

But if one is in the final Testification of Faith of the prayer (at the end of the last rak'a), one says, instead of the above: *Allāhumma ṣalli 'alā Sayyidinā Muḥammadin wa 'alā āli Sayyidinā Muḥammadin kamā ṣallayta 'alā Sayyidinā Ibrāhīma wa 'alā āli Sayyidinā Ibrāhīm(a), wa bārik 'alā Sayyidinā Muḥammadin wa 'alā āli Sayyidinā Muḥammadin kamā bārakta 'alā Sayyidinā Ibrāhīma wa 'alā āli Sayyidinā Ibrāhīma fi l-'ālamīn(a), innaka ḥamīdun majīd* (10.26) ("O Allah, bless our liegelord Muhammad and the folk of our liegelord Muhammad as You blessed our liegelord Ibrahim and the folk of our liegelord Ibrahim. O Allah, show grace to our liegelord Muhammad and the folk of our liegelord Muhammad as You did to our liegelord Ibrahim and the folk of our liegelord Ibrahim in the worlds, for You are truly all praiseworthy and noble").

(17) One closes the prayer with Salams, turning one's head to the right and saying, *As-Salāmu 'alaykum wa raḥmatu Llāh* (10.27) ("Peace be upon you and the mercy of Allah"), intending finishing the prayer, and then turning to the left and saying it again.

The Integrals of Prayer

3.11 The integrals (def: 2.10) of the prayer are:

(a) the intention (def. (1) above);

(b) standing;

(c) the opening Allahu Akbar;

(d) reciting the Fatiha ((5) above), of which *Bismi Llāhi r-Raḥmāni r-Raḥīm* (10.28) ("In the name of Allah, Most Merciful and Compassionate") is a verse;

(e) bowing ((7) above);

(f) straightening back up (8);

(g) prostrating twice (9), sitting back (10) between them;

(h) reposing ((7), second par.) a moment in each position;

(i) the final Testification of Faith (14), sitting therein, and the Blessings on the Prophet (Allah bless him and give him peace) after it (16);

(j) the first of the two Salams which end the prayer;

(k) and the correct order of the above.

Someone unable to stand for the prescribed prayer may perform it sitting, and someone unable to even sit may perform it laying on his side.

The Main Sunnas of Prayer

3.12 The *main sunnas* of the prayer (R: meaning those which if omitted call for a *forgetfulness prostration* (def: 3.16)) are:

(a) the first Testification of Faith (def: (15) above) (R: in prayers that have two);

(b) (R: sitting during it);

(c) the Blessings on the Prophet (16) after it;

(d) (R: the blessings on his folk in the prayer's final Testification of Faith ((16), last par.);

(e) the supplication (qunut) made while standing after bowing in the final rak'a of the dawn prayer (subh) and in the final rak'a of the witr prayer in the second half of the month of Ramadan. (R: It is sunna to lift one's hands and supplicate after straightening up from bowing. One says: *Allāhumma hdinā fī man hadayt(a), wa 'āfinā fī man 'āfayt(a), wa tawallanā fī man tawallayt(a), wa bārik lanā fī mā a'ṭayt(a), wa qinā sharra mā qaḍayt(a)* [here one turns the palms down for a moment]; *fa innaka taqḍī wa lā yuqḍā 'alayk(a), wa innahu lā yadhillu man wālayt(a), wa lā ya'izzu man 'ādayt. Tabārakta Rabbanā wa ta'ālayt* (10.29) ("O Allah, guide us among those You guide, grant us health and pardon among those You grant health and pardon, look after us among those You look after, grant us grace in what You have given us, and protect us from the evil of what You have ordained [turning the palms down for a moment]; for You decree and none decrees against You, none is abased whom You befriend, and none is exalted whom You are at enmity with. O our Lord, who are above all things, sacred and exalted, all praise is Yours for what You decree. I ask Your forgiveness and turn to You in repentance");

(f) (R: and standing during this supplication).

3.13 The other sunnas of the prayer (n: i.e. those whose omission does not entail a forgetfulness prostration) are:

(1) the call to prayer (adhan) and call to commence (iqama) before it;

(2) raising one's hands to shoulder level at the opening Allahu Akbar, before bowing, when straightening up from bowing, and after standing up from the first Testification of Faith (Tashahhud);

(3) placing the right hand over the left (n: between one's navel and one's breast) when standing;

(4) the Opening Supplication (Istiftah, def: 3.10(3)), the Ta'awwudh (3.10(4)), *Āmīn* after the Fatiha, and a sura (3.10(6));

(5) reciting to oneself or aloud, according to the time of day (def: 3.10(6), end), though a woman does not recite aloud in the presence of a man;

(6) saying *Allāhu akbar* in movements from one prayer posture to another (dis: 3.10(7), fourth par.)); saying *Sami'a Llāhu li man ḥamidah* ("Allah hears him who praises Him") when straightening up (3.10(8), second par.); and saying *Subḥāna Rabbiya* etc., when bowing (def: 3.10(7), end) and prostrating (3.10(9), end);

(7) placing the hands on the thighs in the Testification of Faith (Tashahhud), the fingers of the left extended and held together, the right closed with its thumb touching the side of the index finger, which alone is left extended;

(8) sitting in *iftirash* style (3.10(10)) between prostrations and for the first Testification of Faith (Tashahhud), and in

tawarruk style (3.10(14)) in the last;

(9) saying Salams (3.10(17)) to the left after having closed the prayer by saying them to the right, and having the intention of finishing the prayer;

(10) for men to keep their elbows out, and stomach off their thighs in prostration (R: though women keep them close).

The Conditions of Prayer

3.14 The conditions of the prayer are:

(a) that one be Muslim;

(b) that one be free of ritual impurity (def: 3.7(a)), and physical impurity in body, clothes, and place of prayer (3.7(b));

(c) that one clothe one's nakedness, meaning, for a man, what is between the navel and knees, and for a woman, everything besides her face and hands;

(d) knowing the prayer's time has come;

(e) facing the direction of prayer (3.7(e)), other than in the prayer of peril (3.23) or supererogatory prayer when travelling;

(f) that one avoid saying anything other than the words of the prayer, actions other than those of the prayer, and things that break the fast (5.1(b));

(g) and that one's intention (n: of performing the prayer) not change.

3.15 If something happens to one during the prayer (R: such as someone asking permission to enter, or having to remind the imam that he has forgotten something in his Koran recital) then if one is male, one says *Subḥān Allāh* (R: intending only invocation (dhikr) thereby, as one may not merely intend to inform, or lack any particular intention thereby, for these invalidate the prayer), or if female, one claps (R: the right palm on the back of the left hand, not palm to palm).

The prayer is invalidated by omitting an integral (def: 3.11) or condition (3.14).

The Forgetfulness Prostration

3.16 The forgetfulness prostration is sunna (n: not obligatory) and consists of two prostrations performed just before one's closing Salams (n: when one has absentmindedly done something that calls for it).

One performs it for unintentionally doing an uncalled-for action of the type which when done intentionally invalidates the prayer (n: such as a small amount of extraneous speech, or adding an integral or main sunna at the wrong point in the prayer) (R: provided it is not the type of action whose *unintentional* performance also invalidates the prayer, such as *much* (i.e. more than six words of) extraneous speech or action (i.e. more than two consecutive movements), since doing these would in any case invalidate the prayer, and obviate the need for a forgetfulness prostration).

One also performs it for omitting a main sunna (def: 3.12), though not for omitting other sunnas (def: 3.13).

If one remembers (n: missing) an integral (def: 3.11), one goes back to it, performs it, and what comes after it, provided the time was not long (n: meaning if one did not yet reach the same integral in the following rak'a, for in the latter case one simply continues, and the previous rak'a with the missing integral does not count, for if one misses an integral one must perform it, either by going back (if still in the same rak'a) or by performing an additional rak'a (if one has gone on to the subsequent rak'a before noticing the omission) in both cases prostrating for forgetfulness at the end of one's prayer).

If one is unsure one has performed the prayer's full number of rak'as, one presumes that one has done the least number one is certain of, performs the rest, and then prostrates for forgetfulness before closing with Salams.

Group Prayer

3.17 To perform the prayer in a group—other than the Friday prayer (n: which is personally obligatory)—is communally obligatory (def: 1.10(2)) and must be intended as such by the follower at group prayer. The follower must not stand farther forward towards the qibla than his imam. He must know the imam is praying (n: whether by seeing or hearing him, hearing his amplified voice, or seeing a row of those praying behind him, for example). When not in a mosque, the follower must draw near to the imam, and there must not be a barrier (n: preventing passing to him or seeing him) between them.

A boy may lead adults at prayer as imam, though a woman may not lead men, or an unlettered person (n: "unlettered" meaning in this context someone who omits or mispronounces a letter or more of the Fatiha) lead someone who can recite (n: it correctly).

(R: The group prayer is valid:

(1) when the imam is performing a supererogatory prayer and the follower is performing a prescribed prayer, or vice versa;

(2) when the imam is performing the noon prayer (dhuhr) and the follower is praying the dawn prayer (subh) (i.e. when the type of prayer differs) or vice versa;

(3) when the imam is praying while sitting and the follower is praying standing, or vice versa;

(4) when the imam is performing a makeup prayer and the follower is performing a current one, or vice versa.

But a person shortening his prayer because of travelling may not pray behind an imam who is performing the full number.)

Shortening or Joining Prayers for Travel or Rain

3.18 (R: The two travel dispensations of shortening and joining prayers have no effect on each other: one may take both together, either, or none. It is superior in our school not to take dispensations that are permissible.).

It is permissible to shorten current prescribed prayers of four rak'as (R: noon (dhuhr), midafternoon ('asr), and nightfall ('isha)) to two rak'as each, provided:

(a) that one is on a journey of at least 16 *farsakh*s (R: approximately 81 km./ 50 mi. one way);

(b) that one is travelling for a reason that is not disobedience to Allah (R: as there is no dispensation to shorten prayers on such a trip);

(c) (R: that the destination is known (n: from the beginning of the journey, for otherwise, one may not shorten until having actually travelled the distance that permits shortening));

(d) (R: that the prayer takes place from start to finish while on the trip, for if one's vehicle arrives before the prayer is finished, one prays the full number);

(e) and that one intends shortening at the prayer's opening Allahu Akbar.

(R: One may also shorten the above prayers when one both misses them and makes them up on the trip, though one must pray the full number if one misses them while not travelling and makes them up on the trip, or misses them on the trip and makes them up while not travelling.

If one's city has walls, one may begin shortening prayers as soon as one has passed them, whether or not there are other buildings outside them. If there are no walls, one may shorten one's prayers after passing beyond the last buildings, excluding farms, orchards, and cemeteries. When the buildings of one city extend to the next city, one's journey begins at the first's city limits, or what people commonly acknowledge to be "the edge of town."

When the trip ends, one must pray the full number of rak'as for each prayer. A trip *ends* when one reaches one's hometown. It also ends: by the mere intention to stay in a place at least 4 full days, not counting the day one arrives or the day one departs; or by staying that long without the intention, so that after one has stayed 4 full days, not counting the days of arrival and departure, one prays the full number of rak'as, unless one is staying in a place in order to fulfill a purpose that one expects to accomplish and intends to leave as soon as one does. As long as this is the case, one may shorten one's prayers for up to 18 days. If longer than this, one prays the full number.)

Joining Prayers

3.19 It is permissible to join the noon prayer (dhuhr) and midafternoon prayer ('asr) during the time of either of them (R: or the Friday prayer (jum'a) and midafternoon prayer in the time of the Friday prayer), and permissible to similarly join the sunset prayer (maghrib) and nightfall prayer ('isha) during the time of either, when the conditions are met.

(R: The conditions for joining two prescribed prayers on a trip in the time of the first of them are:

(a) that the trip continue until one finishes both prayers;

(b) that the first of the two be prayed first;

(c) that the intention to join the two prayers occur before finishing the first, either coinciding with the opening Allahu Akbar, or occurring during the prayer;

(d) and that one not separate the two prayers by waiting between them, though a short interval, meaning one that could contain two rak'as of the briefest possible, is of no consequence.

If one has performed both prayers and the journey subsequently ends, whether in the time of the first prayer or the time of the second, they are and remain valid.

The necessary condition for joining two prayers in the time of the second of them (in addition to conditions 3.18(a,b,c,d)) is that one make the intention to do so before the end of the first prayer's time by an interval which could contain at least one rak'a. If one neglects this intention, one has sinned, and praying the first prayer during the second prayer's time is considered making it up.)

3.20 A nontraveller may join prayers, when it is raining, in the time of the first of them. (R: It is permissible for a non-traveller to pray the noon prayer (dhuhr) and the midafternoon prayer ('asr) at the time of the noon prayer (or the Friday prayer (jum'a) and midafternoon prayer at the time of the Friday prayer), and to similarly pray the sunset prayer (maghrib) and nightfall prayer ('isha) at the time of the sunset prayer if:

(a) it is raining hard enough to wet one's clothing (and like rain in this is melted snow or hail);

(b) one is praying with a group in a mosque or other place of prayer;

(c) the mosque is far from one's door (n: *far* meaning it would ordinarily be described as such by someone talking about it);

(d) it is raining when the first prayer begins, when it ends, and when the second prayer begins;

(e) and conditions 3.19(b,c,d) exist.

If the rain stops after one finishes the two prayers or during the second one, both prayers are and remain valid.

It is not permissible to join to prayers in the time of the second of them because of rain.)

Other Reasons for Joining Prayers

3.21 (R: In the Shafi'i school, there are no valid reasons other than travel or rain for joining prayers, though others exist in the Hanbali school, as discussed in what follows.)

('Abd al-Rahman al-Jaziri:) The Hanbalis hold that the above-mentioned joining between the noon prayer (dhuhr) and midafternoon prayer ('asr), or between the sunset prayer (maghrib) and nightfall prayer ('isha) is permissible, whether in the time of the first prayer of each of these two pairs, or in the time of the second prayer of each of them, though it is superior not to join them . . . .

It is a necessary condition for the permissibility of joining them that the person praying be:

(1) a traveller on a trip in which shortening prayers is permissible;

(2) a sick person for whom not to join prayers would pose a severe hardship;

(3) . . . or someone who fears for himself, his property, or his reputation, or who fears harm in earning his living if he does not join prayers; the latter giving leeway to workers for whom it is impossible to leave their work.

(*al-Fiqh 'ala al-madhahib al-arba'a* (9.11), 1.487)

Praying Sunna Rak'as When Joining Prayers

3.22 (R: When one wants to join the midafternoon prayer ('asr) and noon prayer (dhuhr) in the time of the noon prayer, one first prays the sunnas that come before the noon prayer, followed by the noon prayer, the midafternoon prayer, the sunnas that come after the noon prayer, and then the sunnas that come before the midafternoon prayer.

Similarly, when one joins the nightfall prayer ('isha) with the sunset prayer (maghrib), one prays the sunnas that come before the sunset prayer, and postpones those that follow the sunset prayer until after one has prayed the nightfall prayer, after which one prays the sunnas that come before and after the nightfall prayer, and then *witr*. Their order is sunna.)

The Prayer of Peril

3.23 The prayer of peril (n: for conditions of combat) is of various kinds. If the enemy is in other than the direction of prayer (qibla), (R: the imam divides the Muslim force into two groups:) one group faces the enemy while the other prays a rak'a behind the imam. (R: When the imam rises for the second rak'a, the group makes the intention to cease following his leadership in the prayer and then finishes their second rak'a alone as individuals while the imam remains standing at the beginning of his second rak'a, reciting the Koran and awaiting the second group. Then this first group goes to relieve the others in facing the enemy, and the other come and begin their group prayer behind the imam.) Then the imam leads the second group in a rak'a. Then (R: at the end of this rak'a, when the imam sits in the Testification of Faith (Tashahhud)) the group (R: rises and) performs their second rak'a without him, and (R: when they catch up with him) he closes the prayer with Salams.

If the enemy is in the direction of prayer, the imam arranges them in two rows, opens the group prayer with *Allāhu akbar* then prostrates together with one row (R: the row nearest him) while the other row remains (R: standing) on guard. When the imam and his row stand (R: after their second prostration), the other row performs its own prostrations and rises to catch up with the imam and his row (R: who have remained standing waiting for them).

In actual combat, Muslims may pray however they can (R: walking or riding, facing the direction of prayer (qibla) or not, in a group or individually), even nodding (R: in place of bowing and prostration when they are unable to perform them, nodding more deeply for prostration than for bowing) or riding.

Friday Prayer (Jum'a)

3.24 The Friday congregational prayer (jum'a) consists of two rak'as and is obligatory for every free male Muslim who is legally responsible, not ill, and a resident.

The conditions for the validity of the Friday prayer are:

(a) that its site be located among the dwellings of the community;

(b) that it be performed as a group prayer with a minimum of forty participants for whom it is obligatory;

(c) that it take place in the time of the noon prayer (dhuhr): if its time finishes, they pray it as (n: a makeup of) the noon prayer;

(d) that two sermons (khutba) precede the prayer, in both of which it is obligatory for the speaker:

(1) to stand during, and sit (n: it being obligatory to sit between the two sermons, and sunna to do so during the call to prayer (adhan));

(2) (R: to say *al-Ḥamdu li Llāh* (10.30) ("Praise be to Allah"), this particular utterance being prescribed);

(3) to say the Blessings on the Prophet (Allah bless him and give him peace);

(4) to enjoin godfearingness (taqwa) (R: for which a particular expression is not prescribed, it being sufficient to say "Obey Allah");

(5) to sit between the two sermons (n: as in (1) above);

(6) to recite one verse of the Koran (R: that conveys an intended meaning, such as promise, warning, exhortation, or similar) in at least one of the two sermons;

(7) and to supplicate for believers (R: male and female) in the second of the two sermons (R: which must be for their *hereafter*, as supplications for this world alone do not fulfill the integral).

(R: The following sermon (n: which is recited in Arabic) has been related by two chains of transmission, one ascribing it to Ibn Mas'ud, and the other through him to the Prophet (Allah bless him and give him peace):

Inna l-ḥamda li Llāh. Naḥmaduhu wa nasta'īnuhu wa nastaghfiruh. Wa na'ūdhu bi Llāhi min shurūri anfusinā wa min sayyi'āti a'mālinā. Man yahdihi Llāhu fa lā muḍilla lah(u), wa man yuḍlil fa lā hādiya lah. Wa ash-hadu an lā ilāha illa Llāhu waḥdahu lā sharīka lah, wa ash-hadu anna Muḥammadan 'abduhu wa rasūluh. Ṣalla Llāhu 'alayhi wa sallama wa 'alā ālihi wa aṣ-ḥābih. Yā ayyuha lladhīna antum Muslimūn (10.31) ("Praise is truly Allah's. We praise Him, seek His help, and ask His forgiveness. We seek refuge in Allah from the evils of our selves and our bad actions. Whomever Allah guides none can lead astray, and whomever He leads astray has no one to guide him. I testify that there is no god but Allah alone, without any partner, and that Muhammad is His slave and messenger. Allah bless him and give him peace, with his folk and Companions. O you who believe: fear Allah as He should be feared, and do not die other than as Muslims").

"Yā ayyuha n-nāsu ttaqū Rabbakumu lladhī khalaqakum min nafsin wāḥidatin wa khalaqa minhā zawjahā wa baththa minhumā rijālan kathīran wa nisā'ā. Wa ttaqu Llāha lladhī tasā'alūna bihi wa l-arḥām, inna Llāha kāna 'alaykum raqībā (10.32) ("O people: fear your Lord who created you from one soul and created its mate from it, and spread forth from them many men and women. And be mindful of your duty to Allah, by whom you ask of one another, and to the wombs [that bore you], for verily, Allah is vigilant over you" (Koran 4.1)).

(n: This sermon, recited in Arabic, fulfills conditions (2), (3), (4), and (6) above—the rest may be in any language—and after sitting briefly, one rises and says, *al-Ḥamdu li Llāh,* the Blessings on the Prophet (Allah bless him and give him peace), enjoins the people to fear Allah, and must add a supplication for the Muslims ((e) above), such as saying *Allāhumma-ghfir lil-mu'minīn wal mu'mināt* (10.33) ("O Allah, forgive the believers").

3.25 The sunnas of attending the Friday prayer are:

(1) to perform a purificatory bath (ghusl) before going;

(2) to clean oneself thoroughly (R: i.e. clean the teeth with a toothstick (siwak), trim the nails, remove bodily hair, and eliminate offensive odors);

(3) to wear perfume;

(4) to wear white;

(5) and during the sermon to listen carefully, and to keep the rak'as of greeting the mosque brief.

The Prayer on the Two 'Eids

3.26 The 'Eid prayer consists of two rak'as (n: performed anytime from when the sun is well up until noon on each of *'Eid al-Fitr* at the end of Ramadan and *'Eid al-Adha* on 10 Dhul Hijja). In addition to the opening Allahu Akbar in the first rak'a and the Allahu Akbar for rising from prostration in the second, it is sunna to say *Allāhu akbar* seven times in the first rak'a (R: after the Opening Supplication (Istiftah) and before saying "I take refuge, etc." (Ta'awwudh)) and five times in the second rak'a (R: before saying the Ta'awwudh.

One raises one's hands each time one says *Allāhu akbar.* One invokes Allah Most High to oneself between each Allahu Akbar, (n: saying: *Subḥāna Llāh, wa l-Ḥamdu li Llāh, wa lā ilāha illa Llāh, wa Llāhu akbar* (10.34) ("I glorify Allah's absolute perfection, All praise be to Allah, There is no god but Allah, Allah is ever greatest")) placing the right hand upon the left each time one says this supplication.

It is recommended to recite Qaf (Koran 50) in the first rak'a and al-Qamar (Koran 54) in the second. Or if one wishes one may recite al-A'la (Koran 87) in the first rak'a and al-Ghashiya (Koran 88) in the second. Or one may recite al-Kafirun (Koran 109) in the first rak'a and al-Ikhlas (Koran 112) in the second.)

Then the imam gives two sermons (R: like those of the Friday prayer in integrals (n: though differing from it in (1) not being at the time of the noon prayer, and (2) that it is not obligatory for the imam to stand during them and sit between the sermons.))

It is sunna to recite *Allāhu akbar* (R: in mosques, homes, and the street, from sunset on) the night before each 'Eid until the imam commences the 'Eid prayer with the opening Allahu Akbar.

It is also sunna to recite *Allāhu akbar* after each prescribed prayer from dawn of the Day of 'Arafa (n: 9 Dhul Hijja) until the midafternoon prayer ('asr) on the last of the three days that follow 'Eid al-Adha. (R: One says: *Allāhu akbaru Llāhu akbaru Llāhu akbar, lā ilāha illa Llāh. Allāhu akbaru Llāhu akbar, wa li Llāhi l-ḥamd* ("Allah is greatest, Allah is greatest, Allah is greatest, there is no god but Allah. Allah is greatest, Allah is greatest, praise be to Allah").It is commendable to add to this: *Wa Llāhu akbaru kabīrā(n), wa l-ḥamdu li Llāhi kathīrā(n), wa subḥāna Llāhi bukratan wa aṣīlā(n), lā ilāha illa Llāhu wa lā na'budu illā iyyāh(u), mukhliṣīna lahu d-dīn(a), wa law kariha l-kāfirūn. Lā ilāha illa Llāhu waḥdah(u), ṣadaqa wa'dah(u), wa naṣara 'abdah(u), wa a'azza jundah(u), wa hazama l-aḥzāba waḥdah(u), lā ilāha illa Llāhu wa Llāhu akbar* (10.35) ("Allah is ever greatest. Much praise be to Allah. Glory to Him morning and evening. There is no god but Allah. Him alone we worship, making our religion sincerely His, though the unbelievers be averse. There is no god but Allah alone. He fulfilled His promise, gave victory to His slave, strengthened His army, and vanquished the Confederates alone. There is no god but Allah. Allah is ever greatest").

The Eclipse Prayer

3.27 The eclipse prayer consists of two rak'as, in each of which one bows twice. (R: The minimum is to open with *Allāhu akbar,* recite the Fatiha, bow, straighten up, recite the Fatiha again, bow again, straighten up and remain motionless a moment, prostrate, sit up, then prostrate again. This is one rak'a, comprising standing twice, reciting twice, and bowing twice. One then prays the second rak'a like the first. (n: It is superior, in addition to reciting the Opening Supplication (Istiftah) and Ta'awwudh for the first rak'a, and the Fatiha, to add Koran recital after each time one recites the Fatiha; preferably al-Baqara (Koran 2) for the first recital, Al 'Imran (Koran 3) for the second, (then, in the second rak'a:) al-Nisa' (Koran 4) for the third recital, and al-Ma'ida (Koran 5) for the fourth.)

It is sunna: (1) to prolong one's Koran recital and one's saying *Subḥāna Rabbiya* etc., while bowing and prostrating, (2) to recite aloud in a lunar eclipse, but to oneself in a solar eclipse, (3) and for the imam to give two sermons (R: like those of the Friday prayer, except that here the sermons follow the prayer, as opposed to those of the Friday prayer, which precede it).

The Drought Prayer

3.28 The drought prayer is like the prayer of the 'Eid. (R: When the land is parched or the water supply is cut off or diminished,) the imam orders the people to repent for their sins, restore what belongs to others, and to fast three days. Then on the fourth day (R: while still fasting) they all come out in their work clothes (R: accompanied by those of the women who do not have attractive figures, livestock, men and women advanced in years, infants, and small children) humbling themselves to Allah, and they pray (R: two rak'as like those of the 'Eid), and then the imam preaches (R: two sermons like those of the 'Eid, except that in place of each Allahu Akbar (n: i.e. nine times before the first sermon (khutba) and seven times before the second), the imam says: *Astaghfiru Llāha l-'Aḏhima lladhī lā ilāha illā huwa l-Ḥayya l-Qayyūma wa atūbu ilayh* (10.36) ("I ask forgiveness of Allah Most Great, whom there is no god but He, the Living, the Ever Subsistent, and I repent unto Him.").)

The imam (R: during the sermons) frequently asks Allah's forgiveness (istighfar) and supplicates Allah (du'a).

The Funeral Prayer (Janaza)

3.29 Washing the deceased's body, shrouding him, praying over him, and burying him are a communal obligation (def: 1.10(2)).

3.30 A Muslim martyred in battle fighting non-Muslims is not washed before burial or prayed over. A stillborn fetus is washed (R: before burial) if the miscarriage occurred after the time at which the spirit was breathed into it (R: four months in the womb (n: though if earlier than this, it is only obligatory to bury it)), and is prayed over if it gave a cry (R: sneeze, or cough when it left the mother, or if it moved).

It is sunna to wash the deceased's body an odd number of times, using water infused with lote tree (*Rhamus spina christi*) leaves for the first washing, and with camphor for the last.

If male, it is sunna for the deceased to be wrapped in three (R: washed, not new, white) shrouds (R: without an ankle-length shirt or turban, each shroud covering the whole body). If the deceased is a woman, it is sunna that she be dressed in a wraparound, headcover, and a shift, and that she be wrapped in two shrouds (R: like those used for men).

The Prayer over the Dead

3.31 The obligation of praying over the deceased consists of saying an opening Allahu Akbar with the intention (R: to pray four Allahu Akbars over the particular deceased person as an obligatory act), then reciting the Fatiha, then saying an Allahu Akbar followed by the Blessings on the Prophet (n: like those of the prayer (def: 3.10(16), 3rd par.)), then saying an Allahu Akbar followed by a supplication for the deceased (R: the minimum being *Allāhumma-ghfir li hādha l-mayyit* (10.37) ("O Allah, forgive this deceased")) then saying an Allahu Akbar followed by the prayer's closing Salams.

Burial

3.32 It is obligatory to bury the deceased on his side facing the direction of prayer (qibla). It is sunna that he be buried in a *lahd* (n: meaning a grave with a lengthwise hole dug into the side of (the bottom of) it that faces the qibla, in which the body lies), and that the top of the grave be levelled (R: 1 span, about 23 cm. above the ground), without building (R: a cupola or house) over it or whitening the grave with plaster.

Consoling the Next of Kin

3.33 It is recommended to console (R: all the relatives of the deceased, meaning to enjoin steadfastness and encourage it by mentioning the reward in the hereafter) for (R: approximately) three days after the burial. It is permissible for the bereaved to cry, though unlawful to lament in a raised voice, or rend one's garments.

4

ZAKAT

الزّكاة

CONTENTS:

When Zakat Is Obligatory

4.1 Zakat is obligatory for every free Muslim (R: male, female, adult, or child):

(a) on camels, cattle, and sheep or goats, when one has possessed a *zakat-payable number* (nisab def: 4.3–4) of them for a full lunar year and has been grazing them on unowned open range for the entire year (n: In regard to this latter condition, it is religiously more precautionary and of greater benefit to the poor to follow Imam Malik, who holds that zakat is obligatory whenever one has possessed a zakat-payable number of livestock for a year, whether or not they are work animals, and whether they have been grazed on open pasturage or fed with fodder for the entire year (*al-Sharh al-saghir ʿala Aqrab al-masalik ila madhhab al-Imam Malik* (9.6), 1.592));

(b) on gold and silver (R: or their monetary equivalents) other than jewelry that is for permissible use, and on trade goods, when one has possessed a zakat-payable amount (R: for one year);

(c) and on staple food crops (according to the soundest position), as soon as one possesses a zakat-payable amount of grains and legumes (R: the staple types that people cultivate, dry, and store, such as wheat, barley, millet, rice, lentils, chickpeas, broad beans, grass peas, and Sanaʿi wheat), raw dates, and grapes (R: There is no zakat on fruit except for raw dates and grapes, the zakat on grapes being taken in raisins, and on dates, in cured dates. There is no zakat on vegetables—all of which rulings apply to the farmers who raise the crops. As for those who buy agricultural produce with the intention to sell it, their produce is no longer considered as crops are, but is rather a type of trade goods, and the zakat on it must be paid accordingly).

Zakat on Livestock

4.2 The minimum number of camels on which zakat is

payable is 5 . . . .

4.3 The minimum number of cattle on which zakat is payable is 30 head, for which it is obligatory to give a yearling (R: meaning a male calf in its second year, though a female may take its place, being worth more). The zakat due on 40 head is a two-year-old female that has entered its third year (R: a male will not suffice. The zakat on 60 head is 2 yearling males. Zakat on additional numbers is figured in the same way: on 30 head, a yearling male, and on 40 head, a two-year-old female (according to which of the two alternatives accommodates the last 10 head (dis: 4.5))).

4.4 The minimum number of sheep or goats (n: the Arabic *ghanam* meaning both) on which zakat is payable is 40, on which it is obligatory to pay a *shah*, meaning either a one-year-old sheep (R: in its second year) or a two-year-old goat (R: in its third year). The zakat on 121 sheep or goats is two *shah*s, on 201 sheep or goats is three, (R: on 400 sheep or goats is 4,) and for every additional 100 the zakat is 1 *shah*.

4.5 (R: Numbers of camels, cattle, sheep or goats which are between zakat quantities (i.e. which number more than the last relevant zakat quantity but do not amount to the next highest one) are not counted, and no zakat is due on them.

New offspring of a zakat-payable quantity of livestock that are born during the year are counted for the zakat year their mothers are currently in, no matter whether their mothers survive or die. Thus, if one owned 40 sheep or goats which gave birth to 40 young before the year's end, but then the 40 mothers died, one's zakat on the offspring would be 1 *shah*.)

Zakat on Shared Property and Similar

4.6 Two people pay zakat jointly as a single person if:

(1) (R: they jointly own a zakat-payable amount of livestock or something else such as fruit, grain, money, or trade goods, as when two people inherit it;

(2) or when the property is not jointly owned, but) their

property is mixed (R: as when each owner has, for example, 15 head of cattle of a herd amounting to the zakat minimum of 30) and they share the same place to bed them down, to gather them before grazing, to water or pasture them, or employ the same shepherd, share the same stud, or share the same place to milk them (R: or similar, such as having the same watchman (for orchards and fields), the same drying or threshing floor (for fruit or grain), the same store, or the same warehouse).

Zakat on Gold, Silver, and Other Money

4.7 The zakat-payable minimum for gold is 84.7 grams (R: on which 2.1175 grams (2.5 percent) is due), and for silver is 592.9 grams (R: on which 14.8225 grams (2.5 percent) is due. There is no zakat on less than this). The zakat due on both is 2.5 percent. Zakat is exacted proportionately (2.5 percent) on any amount over these minimums (R: whether the gold or silver is in coins, ingots, jewelry prepared for uses that are unlawful or offensive, or articles which are permanent acquisitions. There is no zakat on gold or silver jewelry that is for permissible use.)

An immediate zakat of 20 percent is due when one finds a gold or silver treasure (R: buried in pre-Islamic times or by non-Muslims, ancient or modern, if it amounts to the zakat minimum and the land is not owned. If such treasure is found on owned land, it belongs to the owner of the land).

Zakat on Crops

4.8 The minimum on which zakat is payable for crops is 609.84 kilograms of net dry weight (R: free of husks or chaff) on which 10 percent (R: of the net dried storage weight) is due if watered without effort (R: as by rain or the like), though if otherwise (R: such as land irrigated by ditches), 5 percent is due. (R: If 50 percent of the water came from each, for example, one would pay 7.5 percent of the crop as zakat, as this is the mean between the above two percentages.). Zakat is exacted proportionally (n: in the percentage appropriate to the method of watering the crop) on any amount over the minimums.

(R: After one has paid zakat once on a crop (n: if one is the farmer (dis: 4.1(end))), there is nothing further due on it (as there is no repetiion of zakat on one's crops when they are in storage, unlike the repetition of it on money), even if it remains in one's possession for years.)

Zakat on Trade Goods

4.9 Trade goods are appraised at the end of the year in terms of the type of money they were purchased with, and if this reaches the zakat minimum (R: 592.9 grams of silver if bought with monetary currency or silver, and 84.7 grams of gold if bought with gold, these being reckoned according to the values of silver and gold existing during the year), one must pay a zakat of 2.5 percent on them.

(R: When the owner buys trade goods that cost (at least) the gold or silver zakat minimum, the year of the merchandise's possession is considered to have begun at the beginning of the gold or silver's zakat year, so that a merchant's zakat is figured yearly on his total business capital and goods.)

The Zakat of 'Eid al-Fitr

4.10 The zakat of 'Eid al-Fitr consists of 2.03 liters (R: of the main staple of the area in which it is given, of the kinds of crop on which zakat is payable (def: 4.1(c)). If the main staple is bread, as in many countries, only *wheat* may be given, and is what is meant by the expression *giving food* here and in all texts below dealing with expiations (The Hanafi school permits paying the poor the wheat's value in *money*, both here and for expiations). It is permissible to give the best quality of the staple food of the area, but not to give less than the usual quality, such as by giving barley where wheat is the main staple), which must be paid by every Muslim, and (n: by that Muslim) for every person he is obliged to support (def: 8.6) (R: such as his wife and family (e.g. his young son, grandson, father, or mother) if they are Muslim and) if he has enough food (R: 2.03 liters per person above his own expenses and theirs) in excess of what he needs to feed himself (R: and those he is obliged to support, in excess of what he needs to clothe them, and in excess of his debts and housing expenses) on the night before the 'Eid and on the 'Eid itself.

(R: It is permissible to give the zakat of 'Eid al-Fitr to deserving recipients anytime during Ramadan, though the best time is on the day of 'Eid al-Fitr before the prayer. It is not permissible to delay giving it until after the day of the 'Eid (that is, one may give it until sunset), and it is a sin to delay until after this, and one must make it up (by paying it late).)

Giving Zakat to Deserving Recipients

4.11 Zakat is distributed among eight categories of recipients, or those of them who are found. (R: It is permissible for the zakat giver to personally distribute his zakat to eligible recipients or to authorize an agent (wakil) to do so.) The eight categories are:

(1) The poor (R: meaning someone who:

(a) does not have enough to suffice himself, such as not having any wealth at all, or having some, but he is unable to earn any, and what he has is insufficient to sustain him to the end of his probable life expectancy if it were distributed over the probable amount of remaining time; *insufficient* meaning it is less than half of what he needs. If he requires ten dirhams a day, for example, but the amount he has when divided by the time left in his probable life expectancy is four dirhams a day or less, not paying his food, clothing, housing, and whatever he cannot do without, to a degree suitable (n: i.e. it would be commonly acknowledged as such) to someone of his standing without extravagance or penury, then he is poor—all of which applies as well to the needs of those he must support (def: 8.6). A mechanic's tools or scholar's books are not sold or considered part of his money, since he needs them to earn his living);

(b) and is either:

—unable to earn his living by work suitable to him, such as a noble profession befitting him, given his health and social position, which inability is considered the same as not having any work. If such an individual were an important personage unaccustomed to earning a living by physical labor, he would be considered "poor." This also includes being able to do work suitable to one, but not finding someone to employ one;

—or is able to earn his living, but to do so would keep him too busy to engage in attaining knowledge of Sacred Law (n: Nawawi notes, "If able to earn a living at work befitting him except that he is engaged in attaining knowledge of some subject in Sacred Law such that turning to earning a living would prevent the acquisition of this knowledge, then it is permissible for him to take zakat (dis: 8.7) because the attainment of knowledge is a communal obligation, though zakat is not lawful for someone able to earn a living who cannot acquire knowledge, even if he lives at a school (*al-Majmu‘* (9.22), 6.190–91)).

But if one's religious devotions are what keeps one too busy to earn a living, one is not considered poor.)

(2) People short of money (R: meaning someone who has something to spend for his needs but it is not enough, as when he needs five dirhams, but he only has three or four. The considerations applicable to the poor person also apply to someone short of money; namely, that he is given zakat if he cannot earn a living by work befitting him, or if he can earn a living but attainment of knowledge of Sacred Law prevents his doing so; though if he is able to earn a living but extra devotions prevent him from doing so, then he may not take zakat).

(3) Zakat workers (R: these include the person collecting

it, the clerk recording what the owners give, the person who matches the payees to the recipients, and the one who distributes it to recipients.

The zakat workers receive an eighth of the zakat funds. If this amount is more than it would cost to hire someone to do their job, then they return the excess for distribution to the other categories of recipients. But if less than the cost of hiring someone, then enough is taken from the zakat funds to make up the difference. All of this applies only if the imam (caliph) is distributing the zakat and has not allotted a fee to the zakat workers from the Muslim common fund (bayt al-mal). If the property owner is distributing the zakat (or if the imam has allotted the workers a fee from the common fund) then the zakat funds are divided solely among the other categories of recipients).

(4) Those whose hearts are to be reconciled (R: so their certainty may increase, or if they are recent converts to Islam and are alienated from their kin. Those to be reconciled include the chief personages of a people (with weak Islamic intentions) whose Islam may be expected to improve, or whose peers may be expected to enter Islam).

(5) Bondsmen who are purchasing their freedom from their owners (R: they are given enough to do so if they do not have the means).

(6) Those who have debts (R: and they are of three types:

(a) A person who incurs debts in order to settle trouble (between two people, parties, or tribes) involving bloodshed (as when there has been a killing but it is not known who the killer is, and trouble has arisen between the two sides) or to settle trouble concerning property (such as bearing the expense when trouble occurs over it) is given zakat even if he is affluent.

(b) A person who incurs debts to support himself or his dependents is given zakat if he is poor, but not if affluent. If he incurs a debt for something lawful but spends it on some thing unlawful, and then repents (and is felt to be sincere in this, and the original reason is known to have been something lawful), then he is given zakat.

(c) And a third type, which (n: given persons X, Y, and Z) is when Z incurs a debt by guaranteeing to X that Y will pay X (n: what Y owes him). If Z finds that neither he nor Y can pay, then Z is given zakat (n: because he has gone into debt in order to guarantee Y's debt), even if the reason Z agreed to guarantee Y was not charity but was rather that Y would pay him back).

(7) Those engaged in Islamic military operations (R: for whom no salary has been allotted in the army roster, but who are volunteers for jihad without remuneration).

(8) And the traveller in need of money (R: meaning one who is passing among us (i.e. through a town in Muslim lands where zakat is collected), whose journey was not undertaken for the purpose of disobeying Allah. If such a person is in need, he is given enough to cover his personal expenses and transportation, even if he has money back home).

4.12 The least that fulfills the obligation of zakat is to give it to three individuals from each category (R: each category of recipients must receive an equal share, one eighth of the total, but one may give particular individuals within a category more or less) (n: though in the Hanafi school, it is valid for the zakat-giver to distribute his zakat to all of the categories, some of them, or to confine himself to just one of them (*al-Lubab fi sharh al-Kitab* (9.16), 1.155))), except for zakat workers (n: who may number less than three, and) (R: who receive only their due wage (dis: 4.11(second par.))).

4.13 It is not permissible to give zakat to a non-Muslim; or to give from the share of the poor to someone who has enough for his needs, whether through owning or being able to earn it (dis 4.11(1(a,b))); or to give to someone one is obliged to support (R: such as a wife or family member (def: 8.6)).

5

FASTING

الصيام

CONTENTS:

Fasting Ramadan

5.1 Fasting (R: Ramadan) is obligatory for every Muslim who is morally responsible (def: 1.1).

Conditions for a Valid Fast

5.2 Fasting is only valid:

(a) if one makes the intention (R: one must make the intention to fast for each day one fasts. If the intended fast is obligatory, then the intention must be specific (as to the fast being for Ramadan, a vow, an expiation, or whatever), and be made in the night prior to dawn);

(b) and if nothing that breaks the fast occurs, including: leaving Islam; a woman's being in her period of menstruation or postnatal bleeding; deliberate vomiting; sexual intercourse; masturbation (R: whether by unlawful means, like one's own hand, or by lawful means, such as the hand of one's wife); a substance in an (R: open) passageway reaching a body cavity such as the stomach, inner ear, rectum, or bladder (R: *substance* excluding odors, and *open* excluding anything else, such as absorbtion through pores. The deliberate introduction of anything besides air or saliva into the body cavity breaks the fast, though if the person fasting does so absentmindedly or under compulsion, it does not break it).

5.3 (R: The following are not required to fast:

(1) a non-Muslim;

(2) a child;

(3) someone insane;

(4) or someone whom fasting exhausts because of advanced years or having an illness from which he is unlikely to recover.

None of the above-mentioned is obliged to fast or to make up missed fast-days, though someone who misses a fast because of (4) above must give 0.51 liters of food (def: 4.10) for each fast-day he misses.)

Making Up Fast Days Missed for an Excuse

5.4 (R: The following are not required to fast, though they are obliged to make up fast-days missed (*making up,* according to our school, meaning that one fasts a single day for each obligatory fast-day missed):

(1) those who are ill (the *illness* that permits not fasting being that which fasting would worsen, delay recovery from, or cause one considerable harm with; the same dispensation applying to someone who needs to take medicine during the day that breaks the fast and that he can

not delay taking until night);

(2) those who are travelling (n: provided that the journey is at least 81 km./50 mi. one way, and that one leaves town before dawn);

(3) a person who has left Islam;

(4) or a woman who is in her menses or period of postnatal bleeding.

If the ill person or traveller take it upon themselves to fast, it is valid, though a fast by someone who has left Islam, or a woman in menstruation or period of postnatal bleeding is not valid.

A woman whose period ends during the day of Ramadan is recommended to fast the rest of the day and is obliged to make up the fast (and the fast-days prior to it missed during her period or postnatal bleeding).)

Sunnas of Fasting

5.5 The sunnas of fasting include delaying the predawn meal (R: to just before dawn, as long as one does not apprehend dawn's arrival while still eating, though when one does not know when dawn is, it is not the sunna to thus delay it); hastening breaking the fast (R: when one is certain the sun has set. One should break it with an odd number of dates, though if one has none, water is best); and avoiding ugly words (R: slander, lying and foul language, which are always unlawful, but even worse when fasting).

Days Unlawful to Fast

5.6 It is (R: unlawful and) invalid to fast on the two 'Eids or the three days following 'Eid al-Adha. It is also (R: unlawful and) invalid to fast on a day of uncertainty (R: as to whether it is the first day of Ramadan, meaning that on 30 Sha'ban, someone who does not have the necessary qualifications of a witness mentions having seen the new moon of Ramadan), unless it falls on a day one habitually fasts, or is connected with the previous days (R: Fasting on a day of uncertainty is not valid as a day of Ramadan, though it can validly fulfill a vow or a makeup fast. Voluntary fasting on such a day is only valid when one would have fasted any way because it falls on a day one habitually fasts, or when one has been fasting each day since before mid-Sha'ban. If neither of these is the case, then it is unlawful and invalid for one to fast on it.).

Vitiating the Fast by Sexual Intercourse

5.7 Whoever (R: deliberately) vitiates a fast-day by sexual intercourse must make up the fast, and expiate for it as one does for injurious comparison (zihar). (R: The expiation consists of freeing a sound Muslim bondsman, or if not possible, then fasting the days of two consecutive months. (In our school the expiation is only for sexual intercourse, though the Hanafis hold it is obligatory for vitiating the fast for other reasons as well.) If this is not possible, then the expiation is to feed sixty unfortunates (0.51 liters of food (def: 4.10) to each unfortunate). If one is unable to do this, the expiation remains as an unperformed obligation upon the person concerned. The woman made love to is not obliged to expiate it.)

5.8 If someone dies with unperformed fast-days which he could have fasted but did not, then each fast-day is paid for (R: by the responsible family member) with 0.51 liters of food (def: 4.10) (R: or he can fast for him in place of paying for each day. As for someone who dies after two Ramadans elapse upon his missed fast-days, each fast is paid for with 1.02 liters (n: double the above) of food. Or the family member can both fast a day and pay 0.51 liters for each day (i.e. the family member may fast in the deceased's stead for the initial nonperformance of the fast-day, though he cannot fast in place of paying the 0.51 liters of food for each year that making up a fast-day was delayed before the deceased's death, because this is the legal expiation for delaying the fast)).

Valid Excuses from Fasting

5.9 It is permissible (def: 5.4) to omit fasting a day or more of Ramadan (n: and make it up later) if a person is ill, is travelling (R: provided that the journey is at least 81 km/50 mi. one way, and that the person leaves town before dawn), or is a woman who is pregnant or breast-feeding a baby and apprehends harm to herself (R: or her child), though if she omits it because of fear of harm for the child (R: alone, not for herself), then in addition to making up each day, she must give 0.51 liters of food (def: 4.10) in charity for each day missed, as an expiation.

Spiritual Retreat (I'tikaf)

5.10 Spiritual retreat in the mosque (i'tikaf) is a sunna (R: at any time), and is only valid by staying (R: for more than the least amount of time that can be considered *repose,* i.e. a moment) in a mosque with the intention of spiritual retreat. If one vows to make spiritual retreat for a consecutive period, the consecutiveness of such a period is nullified by lovemaking, though not by leaving (R: for something necessary such as eating (even when it is possible to do so in the mosque), drinking (provided it is not possible to do so in the mosque) (n: or)) to use the lavatory, or because of the onset of menstruation, or an illness with which remaining in the mosque presents a hardship.

6

THE PILGRIMAGE (HAJJ)

الحج والعمرة

CONTENTS:

Who Must Perform Hajj and ‘Umra

6.1 (R: Both hajj (n: the pilgrimage to Mecca) and ‘umra (n: the “lesser pilgrimage” (def: 6.3)) are obligatory, though neither is obligatory more than once in a person’s lifetime unless one vows more than that.) Hajj (n: as well as ‘umra) is only obligatory when one is a Muslim who is morally responsible (def: 1.1) and able to afford provisions and transportation (R: round trip, with money one has that is in excess of the amount one requires to support the members of one’s family (def: 8.6) and clothe them while one is travelling there and back, and to obtain lodgings for oneself;

and that is in excess of any money one owes for debts), when the way is safe (R: for one's person and property from predators and enemies), and one is fit enough to travel (R: there without serious harm).

The Integrals of Hajj

6.2 The integrals of hajj are:

(a) entering *ihram* (n: the state of consecration that pilgrims enter for hajj and 'umra) by making the intention (R: When one wishes to enter ihram, it is recommended (even for a woman in menstruation) to perform the purificatory bath (ghusl), intending bathing for ihram. If there is not much water, one merely performs ablution (wudu).

It is also recommended to shave pubic hair, pluck the underarms, clip the mustache, trim the nails, clean oneself of dirt, and wash the head.

Then, if male, one:

(1) sheds any garments that have sewing in them (taking them off being obligatory for ihram, which is incomplete if one does not remove them before entering it);

(2) puts on a clean white mantle (Ar. rida', the rectangular piece of cloth worn over the shoulders that covers the upper body of a man in ihram) and wraparound (izar, the cloth worn around the lower body), and sandals that do not enclose the foot, but rather reveal the toes and heels, as opposed to sandals that cover the toes, for wearing such sandals obliges one to slaughter;

(3) and it is recommended to perfume the body, though not one's clothes.

The above measures (1,2,3) apply equally to women, although women do not divest themselves of sewn garments, a woman being obliged to cover all of her body except the face and hands (n: it is not permitted for a woman to veil her face in ihram), which, in ihram as well as in prayer, are not considered nakedness. But women do not use perfume.

All of the foregoing are done before entering ihram.

One then prays two rak'as, provided it is not a time when the prayer is forbidden (def: 3.3), intending the sunna of ihram. It is sunna to recite al-Kafirun (Koran 109) in the first rak'a, and al-Ikhlas (Koran 112) in the second. Then one rises to start travelling to Mecca. As soon as one begins travelling to Mecca, one has entered ihram.

One intends in one's heart to perform the hajj for Allah Most High, if one wants to perform hajj; or to perform 'umra if one wants to; or both together if one wants to perform them simultaneously (qiran). It is recommended that one also pronounce this intention with the tongue);

(b) standing at 'Arafa (n: a plain about 21 kilometers to the east-southeast of Mecca) (R: at some point between the noon prayer (dhuhr) on 9 Dhul Hijja and dawn of the following day. It is sunna to remain at 'Arafa until sunset so as to include both night and day);

(c) circumambulating the Kaaba seven times (n: among the conditions for which are that one's nakedness (def: 3.7(c)) be clothed, that one have ritual purity from minor (hadath) and major (janaba) impurity, and that each round begin from the Black Stone and that one pass by all of the stone with all of one's body, for if one begins from another part of the Kaaba, the round does not count until one reaches the stone, from whence it begins);

(d) going between Safa and Marwa (R: two hillocks connected by a course adjoining al-Masjid al-Haram) seven times (n: one must begin at Safa and finish at Marwa (R: from Safa to Marwa equals one, from Marwa to Safa is another one, and so on);

(e) and shaving (R: or shortening) the hair (R: men have their entire head shaved, which is optimal, though one may confine oneself to removing (by any means) three hairs thereof (i.e. of the head, not something else such as the beard or mustache), or may merely shorten it, for which the optimal is to clip a little less than two centimeters from all the hair. As for women, it is optimal for them to shorten their hair in the latter way, it being offensive for a woman to shave her head).

The Integrals of 'Umra

6.3 The above are also the integrals of 'umra, other than standing at 'Arafa (n: which is not an 'umra integral).

The Requisites (Wajibat) of Hajj

6.4 The requisites (wajibat) of the hajj are:

(a) that one enter ihram at the proper site (R: people going to hajj from the West by plane must enter ihram before boarding it, or during the flight before it passes the airspace that is even with the city of Rabigh on the west coast of the Arabian Peninsula, this generally being announced on the plane. Medina residents (or those travelling through Medina to Mecca) enter ihram at Dhul Hulayfa (n: often called Abar 'Ali). Residents of the Syria-Palestine region, Egypt, and North Africa enter ihram at al-Juhfa; residents of al-Tihama in Yemen enter ihram at Yalamlam; residents of the Najd of Yemen and the Najd of the Hijaz enter ihram at Qarn; and residents of Iraq and Khurasan (n: the lands east of Iraq) enter ihram at Dhat 'Irq, preferably at al-'Aqiq. Someone at Mecca, even if merely passing through, enters ihram for hajj in Mecca, and for 'umra must go at least to the nearest place outside of the Sacred Precinct (Haram) (n: most people now find it convenient to go to the Mosque of 'A'isha, at al-Tan'im). Someone intending hajj, 'umra, or both, who passes the ihram site (intentionally, absentmindedly, or in ignorance of it) and enters ihram somewhere closer to Mecca, is obliged to slaughter (def: 6.6), though if he returns to the proper site and enters ihram there before having performed a single rite, he is no longer obliged to slaughter);

(b) stoning the stoning sites at Mina (n: i.e. the site of Jamrat al-'Aqaba on 'Eid al-'Adha, and then stoning the three sites on the days after the 'Eid (Ayam al-Tashriq). The conditions for the validity of stoning each site are: (R: that seven pebbles be used; that they be thrown one by one; that one's action may be termed *throwing*, not merely putting the pebbles into the throwing place; that what is thrown be some form of stone; that it be done with the hand; that one aim at the throwing place; that one be certain that the pebble reaches it, even if it falls out again, for if one doubts that the stone reached it, then that stone does not count; (the above seven conditions hold for both 'Eid al-Adha and for the days following the 'Eid, though the days following the 'Eid require two additional conditions:) that the stoning be done after the time for the noon prayer arrives; and that one stone the three sites in the proper sequence (n: i.e. Jamrat al-Kubra, then Jamrat al-Wusta, then Jamrat al-'Aqaba, which was previously stoned with seven pebbles on 'Eid al-Adha)));

(c) spending the night (n: both at Muzdelifa on the night before 'Eid al-Adha, and at Mina on the days following the 'Eid (Ayam al-Tashriq) (R: the obligation to be present at Muzdelifa can be met by coming there, even for a brief moment, during the second half of the night, for *spending the night* merely means to be present there during the second half of the night, not actually staying overnight, as opposed to spending the night at Mina, which must be for the greater part of the night);

(d) and performing the farewell circumambulation (n: just before one leaves Mecca.) (R: The integrals and conditions of the farewell circumambulation are the same as the obligatory circumambulation (def: 6.2(c))).

(R: in the Shafi'i school there is no difference between obligatory (fard) and requisite (wajib) except in the pilgrimage, where nonperformance of a requisite does not invalidate the pilgrimage, but necessitates an expiation (dis: 6.7))

The Sunnas of Hajj

6.5 The sunnas of hajj are:

(1) for one's hajj to precede one's 'umra (n: for that particular year);

(2) (n: for males) to wear a white mantle and wraparound (dis: 6.2(a(2)));

(3) to chant "Labbayk" (n: which is: *Labbayka Llāhumma labbayk, Labbayka lā sharīka laka labbayk, inna l-ḥamda wa n-ni'mata laka wa l-mulk, lā sharīka lak* (three times) (10.38) ("Ever at Your service, O Allah, ever at Your service. Ever at Your service, You have no partner, ever at Your service. Verily, all praise, blessings, and dominion are Yours. You have no partner")) (R: for the duration of one's ihram, whether standing, sitting riding, walking, lying down, and even in a state of major ritual impurity (janaba), or for a woman in menstruation);

(4) to perform (n: when one arrives in Mecca) the arrival circumambulation (tawaf al-qudum) (n: like other circumambulations in number of rounds and other conditions (def: 6.2(c))) (R: the arrival circumambulation is desirable for anyone who enters al-Masjid al-Haram, whether in ihram or not);

(5) and to pray two rak'as after circumambulation (n: behind the Station of Ibrahim (Maqam Ibrahim)) (R: if one prays there. Otherwise, one may perform the two rak'as (in order of superiority) in the Hijr of Isma'il, al-Masjid al-Haram, the Sacred Precinct (Haram), or whenever and wherever one wishes to pray them, and they remain a current performance until the day one dies).

Omitting a Requisite of Hajj

6.6 Leaving a requisite (wajib, def: 6.4) unperformed obliges one to slaughter a *shah* (def: 4.4) (R: distributing its meat to the poor and those short of money (4.11(1,2)) in the Sacred Precinct). If one is unable to (R: slaughter for lack of money while on the hajj, even if one has enough money back home), one fasts three days before 'Eid al-Adha and seven days after returning to one's country.

Missing Standing at 'Arafa

6.7 Someone who misses standing at 'Arafa (R: has missed the hajj, and) releases himself from ihram by performing the rites of 'umra (R: that is, by circumambulating, going between Safa and Marwa, and cutting his hair, and he is thus released from his ihram), and must make up the hajj (n: in a later year) and slaughter (n: or fast, as described in 6.6).

Someone prevented by others from (R: entering Mecca and) completing the integrals of hajj or 'umra after having entered ihram releases himself from ihram by intending release from it, shaving his head, and slaughtering a sacrifice animal (R: at the place he has been prevented).

Things Unlawful in Ihram

6.8 The things unlawful while in ihram include:

(1) sewn garments (R: on men);

(2) men covering the head, or women the face;

(3) applying oil to the hair (R: the beard or scalp);

(4) (R: using perfume;

(5) removing hair or nails;

(6) sexual foreplay;

(7) sexual intercourse;

(8) and hunting).

Committing these (n: any of (1) through (6) while in ihram) entails an expiation of (n: whichever alternative one wishes): (a) slaughtering a *shah* (n: as described in 6.6 above); (b) fasting three days (R: even if nonconsecutive, wherever one wishes); (c) or giving 1.015 liters of wheat to each of six of the poor (R: or those short of money at the Sacred Precinct (Haram)); (n: while (7) and (8) are mentioned next.)

Spoiling the Hajj by Sexual Intercourse

6.9 If one intentionally has sexual intercourse (R: before

finishing one's 'umra, or while on hajj) then:

(a) this nullifies the hajj or 'umra;

(b) it is nonetheless obligatory to complete (R: the hajj or 'umra from the point it was spoiled to the end);

(c) it is obligatory to make it up (R: as soon as possible, even if the spoiled hajj or 'umra was merely supererogatory;

(d) and it is obligatory to pay the expiation (def: below) for the male. If the woman was unwilling, none of the above ((a), (b), (c), or (d)) apply to her, though if willing, (a), (b), and (c) apply to her but not (d)).

The expiation is to slaughter (R: and distribute to the poor of the Sacred Precinct, immediately):

—a camel (R: but if this is not possible within the days of the hajj), then one must slaughter:

—a cow, but if not possible, then:

—seven *shahs* (def: 4.4), but if not possible, then:

—one estimates the cost of a camel and how much food (def: 4.10) this would buy, and then gives that much food (R: to the poor in Mecca) but if not possible, then:

—one fasts one day for every 0.51 liters of food that would have been given had the previous alternative been done (R: one may fast anywhere, but it is not permissible to delay it without an excuse).

Expiation for Hunting

6.10 It is unlawful when in either ihram or the Sacred Precinct (Haram) to kill a game animal, and this necessitates an expiation of (R: any of the following):

(1) to slaughter a head of domestic livestock that is like the wild animal killed (R: *like* meaning an approximation, not actual resemblance. One expiates a game animal that was, for example, large, small, healthy, diseased, fat, thin, or defective, with a head of livestock of the same description, heeding the correspondences);

(2) to estimate the value of the like head of livestock, and distribute an equal value of food (def: 4.10) to the poor;

(3) or to fast one day for every 0.51 liters of food that would have been bought had (2) been done.

7

SUFISM

التصوف

CONTENTS:

The Rules of the Sufi Way

7.1 The basic rules of the way of Sufism are five: (1) having godfearingness privately and publicly, (2) living according to the sunna in word and deed, (3) indifference to whether others accept or reject one, (4) satisfaction with Allah Most High in scarcity and plenty, and (5) turning to Allah in happiness or affliction.

(1) Godfearingness is attained by scrupulousness and uprightness;

(2) Following the sunna is attained through caution and good character;

(3) Indifference to others' acceptance or rejection is attained through patience and trust in Allah;

(4) Satisfaction with Allah is attained through contentment with what one has and submission to the will of Allah;

(5) Turning to Allah Most High is attained by gratitude to Him in happiness and taking refuge in Him in affliction.

The Foundations of the Rules

7.2 The foundations of all of these consist of five things: (1) high aspiration, (2) keeping Allah's reverence, (3) giving the best of service, (4) keeping one's spiritual resolves, and (5) esteeming Allah's blessings.

(1) Whoever's aspiration is high, his rank rises;

(2) Whoever reveres Allah, Allah maintains his respect;

(3) Whoever's service is goodly is necessarily shown generosity;

(4) Whoever keeps his spiritual resolves continues to have guidance;

(5) Whoever esteems Allah's blessings will be grateful for them, and whoever is grateful for them will necessarily see them increased.

The Signs of Sufism

7.3 The principles of Sufism's signs on a person are also five: (1) seeking Sacred Knowledge in order to perform Allah's command; (2) keeping the company of sheikhs and fellow disciples in order to see with insight; (3) forgoing both dispensations from religious obligations and figurative interpretations of scripture, for the sake of cautiousness; (4) organizing one's time with spiritual works to maintain presence of heart; and (5) suspecting the self in all matters, in order to free oneself from caprice and be safe from destruction.

(1) Seeking Sacred Knowledge is vitiated by keeping the company of juveniles, whether in age, mentality, or religion, who do not refer for guidance to a firm principle or rule;

(2) Keeping the company of sheikhs and disciples is vitiated by self-deception and concern with the unimportant;

(3) Leaving dispensations and figurative interpretations is vitiated by leniency toward the self;

(4) Organizing one's time with spiritual works is vitiated by looking for more and more supererogatory worship;

(5) Suspecting the self is vitiated by satisfaction at its goodliness and uprightness.

Curing the Ego

7.4 The principles of curing the ego are also five: (1) lightening the stomach by diminishing one's food and drink; (2) taking refuge in Allah Most High from the unforeseen when it befalls; (3) shunning situations involving what one fears to fall victim to; (4) continually asking Allah's forgiveness (istighfar) and His blessings upon the Prophet (Allah bless him and give him peace) night and day with full presence of mind; and (5) keeping the company of him who guides one to Allah (dis: 8.8).

Reaching Allah

7.5 One reaches Allah Most High (dis 8.9) by (1) repenting from all things unlawful or offensive; (2) seeking Sacred Knowledge in the amount needed; (3) continually keeping on ritual purity; (4) performing the prescribed prayers at the first of their times in a group prayer (and praying the confirmed sunnas associated with them); (5) always performing eight rak'as of the nonobligatory midmorning prayer (al-duha), the six rak'as between the sunset (maghrib) and nightfall ('isha) prayers, the night vigil prayer (tahajjud) after having risen from sleeping, and the *witr* prayer (n: an odd-number of rak'as as one's last prayer before dawn); (6) fasting Mondays and Thursdays, and the "full moon [lit. "white"] days" (n: the thirteenth, fourteenth, and fifteenth of each lunar month), as well as the days of the year that are meritorious to fast; (7) reciting the Koran with presence of heart and reflecting on its meanings; (8) asking much for Allah's forgiveness (istighfar); (9) always invoking the Blessings on the Prophet (Allah bless him and give him peace); and (10) persevering in the dhikrs that are sunna in the morning and evening.

These include:

(1) *Allāhumma bika nuṣbiḥu wa bika numsī wa bika naḥyā wa bika namūtu wa ilayka n-nushūr* (10.39) ("O Allah, through You we reach morning, through You we reach evening, through You we live, through You we die, and unto You is the resurrection") [saying this the morning; and in the evening substituting *ilayka l-maṣīr* (10.40) ("unto You is the final becoming") for *ilayka n-nushūr* ("unto You is the resurrection")].

(2) *Aṣbaḥnā wa aṣbaḥa al-mulku lillāhi wa l-ḥamdu lillāhi wa l-kibriyā'u lillāhi wa l-'aḏḥamatu lillāhi wa l-khalqu wa l-amru wa l-laylu wa n-nahāru wa mā sakana fīhimā lillāh* (10.41) ("We have reached morning and the dominion is Allah's, the praise Allah's, the exaltedness Allah's, the immensity Allah's, the creation, the command, the night and day and all that dwells in them Allah's").

(3) *Allāhumma mā aṣbaḥa bī min ni'matin aw bi aḥadin min khalqika fa minka waḥdaka lā sharīka lak, fa laka l-ḥamdu wa laka sh-shukr* (three times) (10.42) ("O Allah, any blessing that has come to me or any of Your creation is from You alone, without partner, so Yours is the praise and Yours the thanks").

(4) *Allāhumma innī aṣbaḥtu ush-hiduka wa ush-hidu ḥamalata 'arshika wa malā'ikataka wa jamī'a khalqika an-naka anta Llāhu lā ilāha illā anta waḥdaka lā sharīka lak, wa anna Muḥammadan 'abduka wa rasūluk* (four times) (10.43) ("O Allah, I hereby take You as my witness, with the bearers of Your Throne, Your angels, and all of Your creation, that there is no god but You alone, without partner, and that Muhammad is Your slave and messenger").

(5) *Raḍītu bi Llāhi rabban wa bi l-Islāmi dīnan wa bi Sayyidinā Muḥammadin ṣalla Llāhu 'alayhi wa sallama nabiyyan wa rasūlā* (three times) (10.44) ("I accept Allah as Lord, Islam as a religion, and our master Muhammad (Allah bless him and give him peace) as prophet and messenger").

(6) *Āmana r-Rasūlu* . . . to the end of the sura (n: i.e. the last two verses of al-Baqara: *Āmana r-Rasūlu bimā unzila ilayhi min Rabbihi wa l-mu'minūn(a), Kullun āmana bi Llāhi wa malā'ikatihi wa kutubihi wa rusulih(i), lā nufarriqu bayna aḥadin min rusulih(i), wa qālū sami'nā wa aṭa'nā ghufrānaka Rabbanā wa ilayka l-maṣīr(u). Lā yukallifu Llāhu nafsan illā wus'ahā, lahā mā kasabat wa 'alayhā ma ktasabat, Rabbanā lā tu'ākhidhnā in nasīnā aw akhṭa'nā, Rabbanā wa lā taḥmil 'alaynā iṣran kamā ḥamaltahu 'ala lladhīna min qablinā, Rabbanā wa lā tuḥammilnā mā lā ṭāqata lanā bih(i), wa 'fu 'annā wa ghfir lanā wa rḥamnā anta mawlānā fa nṣurnā 'ala l-qawmi l-kāfirīn* (10.45) ("The Messenger believes in what has been sent down to him from his Lord, as do the believers: each believes in Allah, His angels, His Books, and His messengers; we make no distinction between any of His messengers. They say, 'We hear and obey; Our Lord, grant us Your forgiveness, unto You is the final becoming.' Allah charges no soul save in its capacity. In its favor is what it has earned, and against it is what it has earned. Our Lord, do not call us to account if we forget or error; Our Lord, laden us not with a burden like that You placed upon those before us; Our Lord, nor what we have not the strength to bear. And pardon us, forgive us, and have mercy on us; You are our Master, so help us against the people of the unbelievers" (Koran 2:285–86)).

(7) *Fa in tawallaw fa qul ḥasbiya Llāhu lā ilāha illā huwa 'alayhi tawakkaltu wa huwa rabbu l-'arshi l-'aḏhim* (seven times) (10.46) ("So if they turn away, say: 'Allah is enough for me, there is no god but He, on Him I rely, and He is the Lord of the Mighty Throne" (Koran 9:129)).

(8) *Fa ṣubḥāna Llāhi ḥīna tumsūna wa ḥīna tuṣbiḥūn. Wa lahu l-ḥamdu fī s-samāwāti wa l-arḍi wa 'ashiyyan wa ḥīna tuḍh-hirūn. Yukhriju l-ḥayya min al-mayyiti wa yukhriju l-mayyita min al-ḥayyi wa yuḥyi l-arḍa ba'da mawtihā wa kadhālika tukhrajūn* (10.47) ("So glory be to Allah, when you reach evening and when you reach morning. And His is the praise in the heavens and earth, and at the coming of night, and when you reach noon. He brings forth the living from the dead, and brings forth the dead from the living, and gives life to the earth after it is dead; thus shall you too be brought forth" (Koran 30:17–19)).

(9) Ya Sin (Koran 36).

(10) *A'ūdhu bi Llāhi s-Samī'i l-'Alīmi min ash-shayṭāni r-rajīm* (three times) (10.48) ("I take refuge in Allah, the All-Hearing, the All-Knowing, from the accursed devil").

(11) *Law anzalnā hādha l-Qur'āna* . . . to the end of the sura (n: i.e. the last four verses of al-Hashr: *Law anzalnā hādhā l-Qur'āna 'alā jabalin la ra'aytahu khāshi'an mutaṣaddi'an min khashyati Llāh(i), wa tilka l-amthālu naḍribuhā li n-nāsi la'alahum yatafakkarūn(a). Huwa Llāhu lladhī lā ilāha illā huwa 'Ālimu l-Ghaybi wa sh-shahādati huwa r-Raḥmānu r-Raḥīm(u). Huwa Llāhu lladhī lā ilāha illā huwa l-Maliku l-Quddusu s-Salāmu l-Mu'minu l-Muhayminu l-'Azīzu l-Jabbāru l-Mutakabbir(u), subḥāna Llāhi 'ammā yushrikūn(a). Huwa Llāhu l-Khāliqu l-Bāri'u l-Musawwiru lahu l-asmā'u l-ḥusnā, yusabiḥḥu lahu mā fī s-samāwāti wa l-arḍi wa huwa l-'Azīzu l-Hakīm* (10.49) ("Had We sent this Koran down upon a mountain you would have seen it humbled, split asunder for fear of Allah. And those similes, We strike them for men, that haply they may reflect. He is Allah besides whom there is no other god; the Knower of the the Unseen and the Visible—He is the Most Merciful and Compassionate. He is Allah besides whom there is no other god; The King, the All-Sanctified, the All-Peaceful, the All-Faithful, the Guardian, the Invincible, the Overmastering, the Exalted. Extolled be Allah's glory above

what they associate! He is Allah, the Creator, the Originator, the Former. To Him belong the most beautiful names. All that is in the heavens and earth extols His glory; and He is the Invincible, the All-Wise" (Koran 59:21–24)).

(12) Al-Ikhlas, al-Falaq, and al-Nas (Koran 112, 113, and 114 [n: the texts of which are given above at 3.10(6)]) (three times).

(13) *Bismi Llāhi lladhī lā yaḍurru ma'a smihi shay'un fi l-arḍi wa lā fi s-samā'i wa huwa s-samī'u l-'alīm* (three times) (10.50) ("In the name of Allah, with whose name nothing is harmed in the earth or sky, and He is All-Hearing, All-Knowing").

(14) *A'ūdhu bi kalimāti Llāhi t-tāmmāti min ghaḍabihi wa 'iqābihi wa sharri 'ibādihi wa min hamazāti sh-shayāṭīna wa an yaḥḍurūn(i)* (three times) (10.51) ("I take refuge in the perfect words of Allah, from His wrath, His punishment, the evil of His servants, and from the whispering of devils, and lest they come to me").

(15) *Astaghfiru Llāha l-'aḏẖīma lladhī lā ilāha illā huwa l-Ḥayya l-Qayyūma wa atūbu ilayh* (three times) (10.52) ("I ask forgiveness of Allah Most Great, who there is no god besides, the Living, the Ever-Subsistent, and I repent to Him").

(16) *Subḥāna Llāhi wa bi ḥamdih* (three times) (10.53) ("I glorify Allah's absolute perfection and extoll His praise").

(17) *Subḥāna Llāhi wa bi ḥamdihi 'adada khalqihi wa riḍā nafsihi wa zinata 'arshihi wa midāda kalimātih* (10.54) (three times) ("I glorify Allah's absolute perfection and extoll His praise with the number of what He has created, the amount of His satisfaction in His person, the magnitude of the weight of His throne, and the plentitude of that by which His words are eked out").

And if one has enough time, one may recite:

(18) *Subḥāna Llāhi wa l-ḥamdu li Llāhi wa lā ilāha illa Llāhu wa Llāhu akbar* (a hundred times) (10.55) ("I glorify

Allah's absolute perfection, Praise be to Allah, There is no god but Allah, Allah is ever greatest").

(19) *Lā hawla wa lā quwwata illā bi Llāhi l-'Aliyyi l-'Aḏḥīm* (10.56) (one hundred times) ("There is no power and no strength save through Allah, the Most High, the Most Great").

(20) *Lā ilāha illa Llāhu l-Maliku l-Ḥaqqu l-Mubīn* (10.57) (one hundred times) ("There is no god but Allah, the Manifest True King").

(21) *Lā ilāha illa Llāhu waḥdahu lā sharīka lah(u), lahu l-mulku wa lahu l-ḥamdu wa huwa 'alā kulli shay'in qadīr* (10.58) (one hundred times or three times) ("There is no god but Allah alone, without partner, His is the dominion, His the praise, and He has power over everything").

(22) *Allāhumma ṣalli 'alā Sayyidinā Muḥammadin 'abdika wa nabiyyika wa ḥabībika n-nabiyyi l-ummiyyi wa 'alā ālihi wa ṣaḥbihi wa sallim* (one hundred times or three times) (10.59) ("O Allah bless our liegelord Muhammad, Your servant, prophet, and beloved, the Unlettered Prophet; and his folk and Companions, and give them peace).

7.6 And in this amount is a sufficiency, for those reached by the divine help, and Allah gives guidance, and guides to the path. Allah is our sufficiency and best to rely on. Ameen.

8

NOTES

ملاحق وتعليقات

CONTENTS:

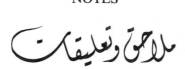

8.1 Notes

8.1 A Warning Against Careless Accusations of Unbelief (from 1.4)

8.1.a (Muhammad 'Alawi al-Maliki:) Many people error, may Allah correct them, in understanding the real reasons that put a person beyond the fold of Islam and necessitate that he be considered an unbeliever . . . .

There is scholarly consensus (ijma', def: 8.3) that it is unlawful to charge with unbelief anyone who faces Mecca to pray, unless he denies the Almighty Creator, Majestic and Exalted, commits open polytheism that cannot be explained away by extenuating circumstances, denies prophethood, or something which is necessarily known as being of the religion, or which is *mutawatir* (n: i.e. the Koran, or those hadiths which like the Koran have been related by whole groups of individuals from whole groups, in multiple contiguous channels of transmission leading back to the Prophet (Allah bless him and give him peace) such that the sheer number of separate channels at each stage of transmission is too many for it to have been possible for all to have conspired to fabricate them, and which are thereby obligatory to believe in and denial of which is unbelief (kufr)), or which there is scholarly consensus (ijma') upon its being necessarily known as part of the religion. *Necessarily known* means such things as the oneness of Allah, the attributes of prophethood, that prophetic messengerhood has ended with Muhammad (Allah bless him and give him peace), the resurrection on the Last Day, the Final Reckoning, the recompense, and paradise and hell—the denier of any of which is an unbeliever, and which no Muslim has an excuse for ignorance of, unless he is a new convert to Islam, who is excused until he can learn, but not afterwards.

To judge a Muslim an unbeliever for anything besides the above is a very dangerous thing, as has come in the hadith,

"If someone says to his fellow Muslim, 'You unbeliever,' one of them deserves the name" [Bukhari, Muslim].

It is not valid for such a judgement to proceed from anyone except someone who knows the things that involve unbelief from those that acquit one of it in the light of the Sacred Law, and the strict demarcation between faith and unbelief according to the standards of the Law of Islam. It is not permissible for any human being to rush onto the field and charge another with unbelief on the basis of opinions and imaginings without having checked and made sure, and without firm knowledge.

. . . Because of this, we urge the utmost caution, in other than the above-mentioned cases, against careless accusations of unbelief, for they are extremely dangerous. And Allah guides to the best of ways, and unto Him is the final destination (*Mafahim yajibu an tusahhaha* (9.15), 5–7).

Deviations and Aberrations That Are Unquestionably Invalid

8.1.b (Muhammad Sa'id al-Buti:) We do not consider *deviations and aberrations* to include any position reflecting a disagreement between Islamic scholars resulting from their differences on derived rulings or particular applications of Sacred Law, for these all return to its basic methodology. Rather, we categorically affirm that this is a normal variance entailed by the very nature of the matter (dis: 8.10) and its methodological bases, though we subject these various viewpoints to an examination of which is the soundest, classifying them according to their relative strengths and weaknesses, each of us through his own reasoning (ijtihad (def: 8.11)) and judgement.

Nor do deviant and aberrant opinions necessarily entail the unbelief of those who hold them, or being beyond the pale of Islam. Rather, there are some opinions so deviant that they reach the degree of negating what is necessarily known as being of the religion, leading to what the Prophet (Allah bless him and give him peace) termed open unbelief; others whose deviance reaches only the degree of being a violation of the methodological principles concurred upon by scholars of the Arabic language and hence by scholars of Islamic Law, entailing blameworthy innovation (bid'a), and perhaps corruption and turning from the truth without excuse; and still others whose deviance and aberrance wavers between reaching actual unbelief and merely falling within the bounds of corruption and blameworthy innovation, the honest and sincere investigator not finding any firm basis to consider them unbelief, yet not being able to accept with confidence that they are only a marginal deviance that does not compromise the person who holds them or put him outside of Islam. In dealing with this category of deviations and intellectual aberrances, we prefer to follow the way of greater precaution, which in this context consists of understanding people's states insofar as possible as if they were still within the fold of Islam and under its rubric. For the mistake of giving them the benefit of the doubt does not entail the losses entailed by making a mistake by not giving them it and accusing them of unbelief and having left Islam. Despite which, we spare no effort to explain their corruption, and that they have innovated something Allah Mighty and Majestic has not given them leave to; explaining their deviation from the methodology agreed upon by the scholars of this Community and warning people not to be misled by them or affected by their falsehoods (*al-Salafiyya marhala zamaniyya mubaraka la madhhab Islami* (9.5), 109–10).

8.2 The Acceptance of Fate (from 1.7)

Things Inconsistent with the Acceptance of Fate

8.2.a (al-Ghazali:) Complaining, no matter what the circumstances, is inconsistent with accepting fate. Criticizing food and finding fault with it is a rejection of what Allah Most High has destined, since blaming what is made is blaming the maker, and everything is Allah's work. For a person to say that "poverty is an affliction and trial," or "having a family to support is a worry and fatigue," or "working for a living is burden and hardship"—all this is inconsistent with accepting fate. One should rather leave the plan to its planner, the kingdom to its king, and say, as 'Umar did (Allah be well please with him), "I do not care whether I become rich or poor, for I don't know which is better for me."

Things Not Inconsistent with the Acceptance of Fate

8.2.b As for prayers (du'a'), Allah requires us to worship Him thereby, as is substantiated by the great many supplications made by the Messenger of Allah (Allah bless him and give him peace) and all the prophets (upon whom be peace). Praying for forgiveness, for Allah's protection of one from acts of disobedience, and indeed for all means that assist one to practice one's religion—none of these is inconsistent with accepting what Allah Most High has destined, for Allah demands the worship of supplications from His servants so that their prayers may bring forth the purity of His remembrance, a humility of soul, and the softening of earnest entreaty so as to polish the heart, open it to spiritual insight, and obtain the manifold blessings of His kindnesses—just as carrying a pitcher and drinking water are not inconsistent with the acceptance of Allah's having decreed thirst. As drinking water to eliminate thirst is merely to employ one of the means that the Creator of Means has arranged, so too is prayer an instrumental relation that Allah Most High has devised and ordered to be used.

To employ such means, in conformity with the normal way Allah Most High deals with the world (sunnat Allah), is not inconsistent with full confidence in divine providence (tawakkul). Nor is hating acts of disobedience, detesting their perpetrators and causes, or striving to remove them by commanding the right and forbidding the wrong; none of which is inconsistent with accepting fate, though some deluded good-for-nothings have erred in this, claiming that since acts of disobedience, wickedness, and unbelief are from the destiny and decree of Allah Mighty and Majestic, accepting them is obligatory—while this is rather from their lack of understanding and blindness to the deep purposes of Sacred Law. For Allah requires that we worship Him by condemning acts of disobedience, hating them, and not acquiescing to them, and blames those who accept them by saying:

"They willingly accept a worldly life and are contented with it" (Koran 10:7);

and

"They accept to remain with the women who stay behind; and a seal has been set upon their hearts" (Koran 9:87).

And in a well known maxim,

"Whoever sees something wrong and accepts it is as though he had committed it."

It might be objected that Koranic verses and hadiths exist about accepting what Allah Most High has destined, while it is impossible and inconsistent with the divine unity that acts of disobedience should not be through Allah's having decreed them, and yet if they are from the decree of Allah Most High, then hating and detesting them is hatred of the decree of Allah, so how can one reconcile these two seemingly contradictory aspects or join between the acceptance and hatred of one and the same thing?

The answer to this is that acceptance and displeasure are only inconsistent when directed towards a single aspect of a single object in a single respect. For it is not inconsistent to dislike something in one respect and accept it in another, as when one's enemy dies who was the enemy of another of one's enemies and was striving to destroy him, such that one dislikes his death insofar as the nemesis of one's enemy has died, yet accepts it in that at least one of them has died. And so too, disobedience has two aspects, one regarding Allah Most High, since it is His effect, choice, and will, in which respect one accepts it out of deference to the Sovereign and His sovereignty, assenting to His disposal of the matter; and another aspect regarding the perpetrator, since it was his acquisition and attribute, the sign of his being detested and odious to Allah, who has afflicted him with the causes of remoteness and hatred, in respect to which he is condemnable and blameworthy.

And this clarifies the Koranic verses and hadiths about hatred for the sake of Allah and love for the sake of Allah, being unyielding towards the unbelievers, hard against them, and detesting them, while accepting the destiny of Allah Most High insofar as it is the decree of Allah Mighty and Majestic (*Ihya' ‘ulum al-din* (9.8), 4.300–303).

8.3 Scholarly Consensus (Ijma‘) (from 1.8)

8.3.a (‘Abd al-Wahhab Khallaf:) Scholarly consensus (ijma‘) is the agreement of all the *mujtahid*s (def: 8.11) of the Muslims existing at one particular period after the Prophet's death (Allah bless him and give him peace) about a particular ruling regarding a matter or event. It may be gathered from this that the integral elements of scholarly consensus are four, without which it is invalid:

(a) that a number of *mujtahid*s exist at a particular time;

(b) that all *mujtahid*s of the Muslims in the period of the thing or event agree on its ruling, regardless of their country, race, or group, though non*mujtahid*s are of no consequence;

(c) that each *mujtahid* present his opinion about the matter in an explicit manner, whether verbally, by giving a formal legal opinion on it, or practically, by giving a legal decision in a court case concerning it;

(d) and that all *mujtahid*s agree on the ruling, for if a majority of them agree, consensus is not effected, no matter how few those who contradict it, nor how many those who concur.

8.3.b When the four necessary integrals of consensus exist, the ruling agreed upon is an authoritative part of Sacred Law that is obligatory to obey and not lawful to disobey. Nor can *mujtahid*s of a succeeding era make the thing an object of new *ijtihad,* because the ruling on it, verified by scholarly consensus, is an absolute legal ruling that does not admit of being contravened or annulled.

8.3.c The proof of the legal authority of scholarly consensus is that just as Allah Most Glorious has ordered the believers, in the Koran, to obey Him and His messenger, so too He has ordered them to obey *those of authority* (ulu al-amr) among them, saying,

"O you who believe: Obey Allah and obey the Prophet and those of authority among you" (Koran 4:59),

such that when those of authority in legal expertise, the *mujtahid*s, agree upon a ruling, it is obligatory in the very words of the Koran to follow them and carry out their judgement.

And Allah threatens those who oppose the Messenger and follow other than the believer's way, saying,

"Whoever opposes the Messenger after guidance has become clear to him and follows other than the believers' way, We shall give him over to what he has turned to and roast him in hell, and how evil an outcome" (Koran 4:115).

8.3.d A second evidentiary aspect is that a ruling agreed upon by all the *mujtahid*s in the Islamic Community

(Umma) is in fact the ruling of the Community, represented by its *mujtahid*s, and there are many hadiths that have come from the Prophet (Allah bless him and give him peace), as well as quotes from the Companions (Sahaba), which indicate that the Community is divinely protected from error, including his saying (Allah bless him and give him peace):

(1) “My community shall not agree on an error”;

(2) “Allah is not wont to make my Community concur on misguidance” [n: Hakim, rigorously authenticated (sahih)];

(3) “That which the Muslims consider good, Allah considers good” [n: Ahmad, from the saying of Ibn Mas‘ud, not of the Prophet (Allah bless him and give him peace)].

(*‘Ilm usul al-fiqh* (9.14), 45–47)

8.3.e (n: Another hadith that scholars quote in connection with the validity of scholarly consensus is the following, given with its commentary.)

The Prophet (Allah bless him and give him peace) said,

“Allah’s hand is over the group, and whoever dissents from them departs to hell.”

Allah’s hand is over the group,

(al-‘Azizi:) al-Munawi says, “Meaning His protection and preservation of them, signifying that the collectively of the people of Islam are in Allah’s fold, so be also in Allah’s shelter, in the midst of them, and do not separate yourselves from them.” The rest of the hadith, according to the one who first recorded it (n: al-Tirmidhi), is

and whoever dissents from them departs to hell.

Meaning that whoever diverges from the overwhelming majority (n: of qualified scholars) concerning what is lawful or unlawful and on which the Community does not differ has slipped off the path of guidance, and this will lead him to hell (*al-Siraj al-munir sharh al-Jami‘ al-saghir* (9.3), 3.449).

8.4 Blameworthy Innovation (Bid'a) (from 1.8)

8.4.a The Prophet (Allah bless him and give him peace) said,

"... Beware of matters newly begun, for every innovation is misguidance."

Beware of matters newly begun

(Muhammad al-Jurdani:) meaning, "Distance yourselves and be wary of matters newly innovated that did not previously exist," that is, invented in Islam that contravene the Sacred Law,

for every innovation is misguidance

meaning that every innovation is the opposite of the truth, i.e. falsehood, a hadith that has been related elsewhere as:

for every newly begun matter is innovation, every innovation is misguidance, and every misguidance is in hell

meaning that everyone who is misguided, whether through himself or by following another, is in hell, the hadith referring to matters that are not good innovations with a basis in Sacred Law. It has been stated (n: by al-'Izz ibn 'Abd al-Salam) that innovations (bid'a) fall under the five headings of the Sacred Law (n: the obligatory, unlawful, recommended, offensive, and permissible):

(1) The first category comprises innovations that are *obligatory,* such as recording the Koran and laws of Islam in writing when it was feared that something might be lost from them; the study of the disciplines of Arabic that are necessary to understand the Koran and sunna such as grammar, word declension, and lexicography; hadith classification to distinguish between genuine and spurious prophetic traditions; and the philosophical refutations of arguments advanced by the Mu'tazilites (n: an early philosophical school that subjected the fundamentals of Islamic faith to rationalistic theories) and the like.

(2) The second category is that of unlawful innovations such as non-Islamic taxes and levies (n: that exceed the amount necessary to prevent the public detriment), giving positions of authority in Sacred Law to those unfit for them, and devoting one's time to learning the beliefs of heretical sects that contravene the tenets of faith (def: 1.1–4) of Ahl al-Sunna.

(3) The third category consists of recommended innovations such as building hostels and schools of Sacred Law, recording the research of Islamic schools of legal thought, writing books on beneficial subjects, extensive research into fundamentals and particular applications of Sacred Law, in-depth studies of Arabic linguistics, the reciting of *wirds* (n: a daily amount of *dhikr*) by those with a Sufi path (def: 7.1), and commemorating the birth (mawlid) of the prophet Muhammad (Allah bless him and give him peace) and wearing one's best and rejoicing at it.

(4) The fourth category includes innovations that are *offensive,* such as embellishing mosques, decorating the Koran, and having a backup man (muballigh) loudly repeat the spoken Allahu Akbar of the imam when the latter's voice is already clearly audible to those praying behind him.

(5) The fifth category is that of innovations that are *permissible,* such as sifting flour, using spoons, and having more enjoyable food, drink, and housing.

(*al-Jawahir al-lu'lu'iyya fi sharh al-Arba'in al-Nawawiyya* (9.12), 220–21)

8.4.b ('Abdullah Muhammad al-Ghimari:) In his *al-Qawa'id al-kubra,* al-'Izz ibn 'Abd al-Salam classifies innovations (bid'a), according to their benefit, harm, or indifference, into the five categories of rulings: the obligatory, recommended, unlawful, offensive, and permissible; giving examples of each and mentioning the principles of Sacred Law that verify his classification. His words on the subject display his keen insight and comprehensive knowledge of both the principles of jurisprudence and the human advantages and disadvantages in view of which the Lawgiver has established the rulings of Sacred Law.

Because his classification of innovation (bid'a) was established on a firm basis in Islamic jurisprudence and legal principles, it was confirmed by Imam Nawawi, Ibn Hajar al-'Asqalani, and the vast majority of Islamic scholars, who received his words with acceptance and viewed it obligatory to apply them to the new events and contingencies that occur with the changing times and the peoples who live in them.

One may not support the denial of his classification by clinging to the hadith "Every innovation is misguidance," because the only innovation that is purely misguidance is in tenets of faith, like the innovations of the Mu'tazilites, Qadarites, Murji'ites, and so on, that contradicted the beliefs of the early Muslims. This is the innovation of misguidance because it is harmful and devoid of benefit.

As for innovation in works, meaning the occurrence of an act connected with worship or something else that did not exist in the first century of Islam, it must necessarily be judged according to the five categories mentioned by al-'Izz ibn 'Abd al-Salam. To claim that such innovation is misguidance without further qualification is simply not applicable to it, for new things are among the exigencies brought into being by the passage of time and generations, and nothing that is new lacks a ruling of Allah Most High that is applicable to it, whether explicitly mentioned in primary texts, or inferable from them in some way. The only reason that Islamic Law can be valid for every time and place and be the consummate and most perfect of all divine laws is because it comprises general methodological principles and universal criteria, together with the ability its scholars have been endowed with to understand its primary texts, the knowledge of types of analogy and parallelism, and the other excellences that characterize it. Were we to rule that every new act that has come into being after the first century of Islam is an innovation of misguidance without considering whether it entails benefit or harm, it would invalidate a large share of the fundamental bases of Sacred Law as well as those rulings established by analogical reasoning, and would narrow and limit the Sacred Law's vast and comprehensive scope (*Adilla Ahl al-Sunna wa al-Jama'a* (9.23), 145–47).

8.5 Transliteration Note

8.5.a (n:) The present volume uses the conventional Arabic transliteration found in American scholarly publications of Middle Eastern studies such those of the University of Chicago Press. It differs from the usual system only in symbolizing the letter ظ as *ḏh̲* instead of *ẓ,* to better represent the classical Arabic pronunciation, and by parenthesizing the final letter where pauses are likely. At such junctures, the parenthesized letter is not pronounced if one pauses, though is pronounced if there is no pause between it and subsequent words. Finally, if in such a case a parenthesized *n* is pronounced after a long *ā,* as for example in the word *kathīrā(n)*, the *a* becomes short.

8.6 Supporting Family Members (from 4.10)

8.6.a (R:) It is obligatory to support the persons listed below, whether one is male or female, when one has money in excess of one's own living expenses and (if male) those of one's wife (meaning enough for a day and night, oneself taking priority over others, followed by one's wife, who takes precedence over other family members):

(1) one's father, father's father, and on up;

(2) one's mother, grandmothers (from either parent's side) and on up;

(3) and one's children, male and female, their children, and on down.

(Money in excess of one's own living expenses and those of one's wife means one is obliged to sell, if necessary to fulfill the obligation to support the above-mentioned persons, whatever must be sold when one has to pay debts, including real estate and other property.)

But supporting the above-mentioned persons is only obligatory when:

(a) there is poverty (a restriction applicable to both support of one's ancestors and one's descendants, meaning that it is necessary in order for it to be obligatory to support one's ancestor that the ancestor be poor, since if he has enough money, one need not support him);

(b) and incapacity to earn a living, whether due to chronic illness, to being a child, or to mental illness. This condition is only applicable to support of one's offspring, not of one's ancestors. If an impoverished ancestor, such as one's father, were able to earn a living from a job suitable to him, it would still be obligatory to support him, and he would not be called upon to earn a living, because of the extreme respect due to him, as opposed to one's descendant, whom one need not support if the descendant is able to earn his own living, but who rather is called upon to do so himself.

The upshot is the support of whoever has enough money for their own support is not obligatory upon another family member, no matter whether the former is mentally ill or sane, a child or adult, chronically ill or well; because he does not deserve charity in such a condition—while a descendant able to earn an adequate living does not deserve support from his ancestors.

8.7 Students of Sacred Law Accepting Zakat (from 4.11)

8.7.a (al-Ghazali:) If someone attaining knowledge of

Sacred Law would be prevented from doing so if he were to engage in earning a living, he is considered “poor” (in respect to the permissibility of his accepting zakat), and his ability to earn is not taken into consideration. But if he is merely a devotee whose gaining a livelihood would busy him from his religious devotions and schedule of supererogatory worship, then he must go earn a living, for earning is more important than devotions.

. . .The second category consists of those who are short of money (miskin), i.e. whose income does not cover their expenses. Someone might possess a thousand dirhams and be “short of money,” while another might possess nothing but an axe and rope and be self-sufficient. The modest lodgings one lives in and the clothes that cover one, to the degree required by one’s condition, do not negate one’s being short of money. Nor do household furnishings, meaning those which one needs and are suitable for one. Nor does possessing books of law negate one’s being short of money (n: if one is a student of Sacred Law accepting zakat, as above), for if one owned nothing but books, one would not be obligated to pay the zakat of ‘Eid al-Fitr (def: 4.10), since books are legally considered as clothing and furnishings are, in that one needs them. One should, however, take the way of greater precaution in curbing one’s need of books. Books are only needed for three purposes: teaching, personal benefit, and reading for entertainment. As for the need of reading for entertainment, it is not considered legally significant such as with books of poetry, historical chronicles, and similar, which are of no benefit in the hereafter and no use in this life except reading and enjoyment. Such books must be sold to pay what is due when one owes an expiation or the zakat of ‘Eid al-Fitr, and someone possessing them is not considered “short of money.” As for the need to teach, if one needs a book to earn a living, as do trainers, teachers, or instructors who work for a salary, such books are the tools of their trade and are not sold to pay the zakat of ‘Eid al-Fitr, nor are one’s books sold if one teaches to fulfill the communal obligation (def: 1.10(2)) of doing so; possessing them does not negate one's being short of money, for this is an important need.

As for personal benefit and learning from books, such as keeping books of medicine to treat oneself or books of pious exhortations to read and take admonition from, if there is a doctor or an exhorter in town, one does not need them, while if there is not, one does.

Further, it may happen that one does not need to read a book except after a time, in which case the period in which one needs it should be stipulated, the most reasonable criterion for which would seem to be that whatever one is not in need of during the course of the year one does not really need, for someone with food in excess of his needs for one day is obliged to pay the zakat of 'Eid al-Fitr, and if we stipulate the need for food as being that of one day, we should consider the need for furnishings and clothing as one year, summer clothing not being sold in winter, for example. Books, clothing, and furnishings would seem to be alike in this. Or someone might have two copies of a book and not need both, such that if he were to say that one is more accurate while the other is of finer quality, so both are needed, we would tell him to be satisfied with the more accurate one and sell the finer, forgoing mere entertainment and luxury. If one has two books on a subject, one of which is comprehensive and the other abridged, then if personal benefit is the purpose, one should keep the more comprehensive, while if one needs them to teach, one may require both, since each possesses a virtue not found in the other.

Similar examples are innumerable and the discipline of jurisprudence cannot cover them all. Rather, the above have been mentioned because of widespread abuse, and to apprise of the merit of the above criterion over others. For it is impossible to deal with all cases, which would entail estimating the amount, number, and kinds of household furnishings and clothes, the spaciousness of a house or lack of it, and so forth, there being no firm limits to such matters.

But the legal scholar must use personal reasoning (ijtihad, 8.11) with respect to them and approximate the criteria that seem likeliest to him, braving the danger of falling into things of doubtful legality, while a godfearing person will take the path that is religiously more precautionary, leaving what causes him doubt for what does not. There are many gray areas between the two clear-cut extremes, and nothing can save one from them except following the way of greater precaution (*Ihya' 'ulum al-din* (9.8), 1.199).

8.8 Taking a Guide to Allah (from 7.4)

8.8.a (n:) In Sufism, as in any other Islamic discipline, be it jurisprudence (fiqh), Koranic recital (tajwid), or hadith, a disciple must have a master or *sheikh*, from whom to take the knowledge, one who has himself taken it from a master, and so on, in an unbroken series of masters back to the Prophet (Allah bless him and give him peace) who is the source of all Islamic knowledge. In Sufi tradition, this means not only that each sheikh has met and taken the way from a master, but that the master during his lifetime has explicitly and verifiably authorized the sheikh—whether in writing or in front of a number of witnesses—to teach the spiritual path as a fully authorized guide (murshid ma'dhun) to succeeding generations of disciples.

Such a chain of transmission (silsila) through an unbroken line of masters is one criterion that distinguishes a true or *connected* Sufi path (tariqa muttasila), from an inauthentic or *dissevered* path (tariqa munqati'a) whose leader, for example, may claim to be a sheikh on the basis of an authorization given by a master in private or under other unverifiable circumstance, or by a figure now passed from this world such as one of the righteous or the Prophet (Allah bless him and give him peace), or in a dream, and so on. These "warm the heart" (yusta'nasu biha) but none meets Sufism's condition that a sheikh must have a clear authorization, connecting him to an unbroken succession of masters of the way, one that is verified by others than himself, without which the way would be open to pretenders.

There are other conditions for sheikhs, reflecting the fact that no one other than prophets are divinely protected from error (ma'sum): a master could conceivably authorize an unworthy candidate as sheikh; or a sheikh might change after his master's death as the result of not having spent sufficient time with him; and so on. Conditions for being a sheikh besides being authorized are described in what follows.

8.8.b ('Abd al-Wahhab al-Sha'rani:) The path of the Sufis is built of the Koran and sunna, and is based upon living according to the morals of the prophets and purified ones . . . .

Sufis unanimously concur that none is fit to teach in the path of Allah Might and Majestic save someone with comprehensive mastery of the Sacred Law, who knows its explicit and implicit rulings, which of them are of general applicability and which are particular, which supersede others and which are superseded. He must also have a thorough grounding in Arabic, be familiar with its figurative modes and similes, and so forth. So every true Sufi is a scholar in Sacred Law, though the reverse is not necessarily true (*al-Tabaqat al-kubra* (9.25), 1.4).

8.8.c (Ahmad Zarruq:) The conditions of a sheikh to whom a disciple my entrust himself are five:

(a) sound religious knowledge;

(b) true experience of the Divine;

(c) exalted purpose and will;

(d) a praiseworthy nature;

(e) and penetrating insight.

Someone with all five of the following is not fit to be a sheikh:

(1) ignorance of the religion;

(2) disparaging the honor of the Muslims;

(3) involvement in what does not concern him;

(4) following caprice in everything;

(5) and showing bad character without a second thought.

If there is no sheikh who is a true guide (murshid, def: 8.8.d), or there is one, but he lacks one of the five conditions, then the disciple should rely on those of his qualities that are perfected in him, and deal with him as a brother (meaning the sheikh and disciple advise one another) regarding the rest (*Qawanin hukm al-ishraq* (9.24), 119).

The Purpose of Taking a Sheikh and a Path

8.8.d (Muhammad al-Hashimi:) As for when the path is merely "for the blessing of it" and the sheikh lacks some of the conditions of a true guide, or when the disciple is seeking several different aims from it at once, or the disciple's intention is contrary to the spiritual will of the sheikh, or the time required is unduly prolonged, or he is separated from his sheikh by the latter's death or the exigencies of the times and has not yet completed his journey to Allah on the path or attained his goal from it—then it is obligatory for him to go and associate with someone who can complete his journey for him and convey him to what he seeks from the path, as it is not permissible for him to remain bound to the first sheikh his whole life if it is only to die in ignorance of his Lord, claiming that this is the purpose of the path. By no means is this the purpose.

The purpose of the path is to reach the goal, and a path that does not reach it is a means without an end. The path was made for travel on it with the intention of reaching one's goal, not for remaining and residing in even if this leads to dying in ignorance of one's Lord. The meaning of a true disciple is one who forthrightly submits himself to a living sheikh during the days of his journey to Allah Most High so that the sheikh may put him through the stages of the journey until he can say to him, "Here you are, and here is your Lord" (*al-Hall al-sadid li ma astashkalahu al-murid* (9.9), 7).

8.8.e (n:) Muhammad Hashimi's above words about submitting oneself to a living sheikh refer to matters within the range of the permissible or recommended, not what contradicts the Sacred Law or beliefs of Islam (def: 8.12), for no true sheikh would ever countenance such a contravention, let alone have a disciple do so, a fact that furnishes the subject of the remaining entries of this section.

8.8.f (Muhyiddin ibn al-'Arabi:) When we see someone in this Community who claims to be able to guide others to Allah, but is remiss in but one rule of the Sacred Law—even if he manifests miracles that stagger the mind—asserting that his shortcoming is a special dispensation for him, we do not even turn to look at him, for such a person is not a sheikh, nor is he speaking the truth, for no one is entrusted with the secrets of Allah Most High save one in whom the ordinances of the Sacred Law are preserved (*Jami' karamat al-awliya'* (9.20), 1.3).

8.8.g (al-'Izz ibn 'Abd al-Salam:) The Sacred Law is the scale upon which men are weighed and profit is distinguished from loss. He who weighs heavily on the scales of the Sacred Law is of the friends of Allah, among whom there is disparity of degree. And he who comes up short in the scales of the Sacred Law is of the people of ruin, among whom there is also disparity of degree. If one sees someone who can fly though the air, walk on water, or inform one of the unseen, but who contravenes the Sacred Law by committing an unlawful act without an extenuating circumstance that legally excuses it, or who neglects an obligatory act without lawful reason, one may know that such a person is a devil Allah has placed there as a temptation to the ignorant.

Nor is it farfetched that such a person should be one of the means by which Allah chooses to lead men astray, for the Antichrist will bring the dead to life and make the living die, all as a temptation and affliction to those who allow themselves to be misled (*al-Imam al-'Izz ibn 'Abd al-Salam* (9.7), 1.137).

The Story of Khidr and Moses

8.8.h (R:) There is sometimes discussion as to whether the story of Khidr and Moses (Koran 18:65–82) does not show that exceptions to Islamic Law are possible. In fact, the verses give no grounds for such an inference, for two reasons. The first is that the context of the story is the time of Moses, not the time of Muhammad (Allah bless him and give him peace), whose Sacred Law is distinguished above that of any of the previous prophets by being final and inabrogable. The second reason is that Khidr, as the vast majority of scholars affirm, was himself a prophet, and his actions were given to him to perform by divine revelation (wahy), this invalidating any comparison between Khidr's exceptionality to the law of Moses and that of any individual born in our own times, for there is no prophet born after the time of Muhammad (Allah bless him and give him peace).

It might be wondered why Allah Most High mentions the story of Khidr and Moses in the Koran at all, if the exceptionality of Khidr was restricted to the time of Moses. The answer is that there is much wisdom in the story, such as that some particular excellence not found in the superior of two things or people may well be found in the inferior of them, for Moses was a prophetic messenger (rasul) while Khidr was only a prophet (nabi); that there are secrets give to certain of Allah's servants which not everyone in the Community (Umma) is responsible to know; that one should learn wisdom wherever one can; and that no matter how much one knows, one should not claim to have knowledge. And Allah knows best.

Sufism and Orthodoxy

8.8.i (‘Abd al-Qadir al-Baghdadi:) The book *Tarikh al-Sufiyya* [The history of the Sufis] by Abu ‘Abd al-Rahman al-Sulami, comprises the biographies of nearly a thousand sheikhs of the Sufis, none of whom belonged to heretical sects and all of whom were of the orthodox Sunni community (Ahl al-Sunna), with the exception of only three of them: Abu Hilman of Damascus, who pretended to be of the Sufis but actually believed in “divine indwelling” (hulul); Husayn ibn Mansur al-Hallaj, whose case remains problematic, though Ibn ‘Ata’, Ibn Khafif, and Abul Qasim al-Nasrabadhi approved of him; and al-Qannad, whom the Sufis accused of being a Mu‘tazilite (def: 8.4.a(1)) and rejected, for the good does not accept the wicked (*Usul al-din* (9.4), 315–16).

8.9 Reaching Allah (from 7.5)

8.9.a (n:) Among the disservices done to Islam by some Western scholars is their tireless insistence that the Sufi term *wusul* (“to arrive, to reach”) be translated as if it meant *ittihad* (“to unify”) with the result that their translations of Sufi works are filled with talk of “union with God,” a rendering that has come to be traditional and authoritative among them, while it is a fallacious conception that the masters of Sufism from every age have taken pains to dissociate themselves, their method, and their students from. So it is perhaps fitting to include in this section with two of the aphorisms of the great Shadhili master Ibn ‘Ata’ Illah, who said:

“Your reaching Allah is reaching the knowledge of Him, for other than that, Our Lord is too exalted for anything to be joined with Him or for Him to be joined with anything”;

and said,

“The affirmation of electhood does not necessitate a negation of the fact of being human. Election is merely like the rise of the daylight's sun: it appears on the horizon without being part of it. Sometimes He takes it from you and returns you to your own bounds. For daylight is not from you to yourself. It comes over you."

(*al-Hikam al-'Ata'iyya wa al-munajat al-ilahiyya* (9.10), 59, 66, aphorisms 213 and 249)

8.10 Why Legal Scholars Differ (from 8.1.b)

8.10.a (Salih Mu'adhdhin:) Muslims of the orthodox Sunni Community (Ahl al-Sunna wa al-Jama'a) are in agreement that we have arrived at all the rulings of Sacred Law through evidence that is either of *unquestionably established transmission* (qat'i al-wurud) or *probabilistically established transmission* (dhanni al-wurud).

The suras of the Koran, all of its verses, and those hadiths which have reached us by so many channels of transmission that belief in them is obligatory (mutawatir) are all of unquestionably established transmission, since they have reached us by numerous means, by generation from generation, whole groups from whole groups, such that it is impossible that the various channels could all have conspired to fabricate them.

As from the evidentiary character of these texts, whether they are of unquestionable or probabilistically established transmission, they are of two types.

The first type, unquestionable as evidence (qat'i al-dalala), is a plain text that does not admit of more than one meaning, which no mind can interpret beyond its one meaning, and which there is no possibility to construe in terms of other than its apparent sense. This type includes Koranic verses that deal with fundamental tents of faith in the oneness of Allah, the prayer, zakat, and fasting; in none of which is there any room for disagreement, nor have any differences concerning them been heard of or reported from the Imams of Sacred Law. Everything in this category is termed *unquestionable as evidence.*

The second type, probabilistic as evidence (dhanni al-dalala), is a text that can bear more than one meaning, whether because it contains a word that can lexically have two different meanings, or because it was made by way of figure of speech or metaphor, or because it can be interpreted in other than its apparent sense in the context without this contradicting what was intended by the Wise Lawgiver. It is here that we find scope for scholarly difference of opinion to a greater or lesser extent depending on the number of meanings a text can imply, how much interpretation it will bear, and so forth.

All of the derivative rulings of Sacred Law are of this type, probabilistic as evidence, so we naturally find differences among Islamic legal scholars as to their interpretation, each scholar interpreting them according to his comprehension and the broadness of his horizons, while not giving the text a reading it does not imply, and then corroborating his interpretation with evidence acceptable to scholars. Scholarly differences are thus something natural, even logically necessary, as a result of the factors we have just described.

Allah Mighty and Majestic has willed that most texts of the Sacred Law be probabilistic as evidence because of a wisdom He demands, namely, to give people more choice and leave room for minds to use *ijtihad* in understanding His word and that of His messenger (Allah bless him and give him peace).

8.10.b We conclude this short summary with an example to clarify what we have said. Consider the word of Allah,

"Divorced women shall wait by themselves for three periods" (Koran 2:228),

as opposed to His saying, in the same sura,

"Those who forswear their women have a wait of four

months" (Koran 2:226).

Allah's saying "three" in the former and "four" in the latter are texts that are decisive as evidence, in that neither admits of more than one interpretation, namely, the well-known numbers.

But in contrast with this, when Allah says "periods" (Ar. quru') in the first, and "months" (ashhur) in the second, we find that the former word can have more than one sense in its Arabic lexical root meaning, while *months* cannot, the latter being decisive in meaning and incapable of bearing another interpretation. Concerning this question, Imam al-Qurtubi says in his Koranic exegesis: "Scholars differ about the word *periods*. Those of Kufa hold that it means menstrual periods, and this is the position of 'Umar, 'Ali, and Ibn Mas'ud. But those of the Hijaz hold it means the interval of purity between menstrual periods, and this is the view of 'A'isha, Ibn 'Umar, and Shafi'i.

Considering this, is it not natural that there should be various opinions about understanding the verse "three periods" but only one about understanding Allah's saying "four months"? If Allah had wanted all opinions to coincide on this question, He might have said, for example, "three menstrual periods" (hiyad), or "three intervals of purity between menstrual periods" (at-har), just as He said "four months." And all the texts of Sacred Law that can bear more than one meaning are comparable to this example (*'Umdat al-salik* (9.18), 11–13).

8.11 The Meaning of *Ijtihad* (from 8.1.b)

8.11.a (n:) To explain the meaning of *ijtihad* or being qualified to issue expert Islamic legal opinion (the person who does this being called a *mujtahid*), the qualifications for an Islamic judge (qadi) have been added below from *The Reliance of the Traveller* (9.13). The difference between the qualifications for the Imam of a school of jurisprudence (madhhab) and those for a judge or mufti is that the former's competence in giving opinion is absolute, extending to all subject matters in the Sacred Law, while the competence of the judge or mufti is limited respectively to judging court cases or to applying his Imam's *ijtihad* to particular questions.

No age of history is totally lacking people who are competent in *ijtihad* on particular questions that are new, and this is an important aspect of Sacred Law, to provide solutions to new ethical problems by means of sound Islamic legal methodology in applying the Koranic and hadith primary texts. Indeed, scholars tell us that if there were no one among the Muslims in a particular age to be apply *ijtihad* in the function of a judge or mufti, the entire community would be guilty of a serious sin. But while in this specific sense the door of *ijtihad* is not and cannot be closed, Islamic scholarship has not accepted anyone's claims to absolute *ijtihad* since Imams Abu Hanifa, Malik, Shafi'i and Ahmad. If one studies the intellectual legacy of these men under scholars who have a working familiarity with it, it is not difficult to see why.

As for those who decry "hidebound conservatism" and would open the gate of *ijtihad* for themselves while lacking or possibly not even knowing the necessary qualifications, if such people have not studied the rulings of a particular school and the relation between these rulings, the Koranic and hadith primary texts, and the school's methodological principles, they do not know how *ijtihad* works from an observer's standpoint, let alone how to employ it. To ask them, for example, which of two equally authenticated primary texts that conflict on a legal question should be given precedence, and why, is like asking an aspiring drafting student for the particulars of designing a suspension bridge. Answers may be forthcoming, but they will not be the same as those one could get from a qualified contractor. To urge that a *mujtahid* is not divinely protected from error (ma'sum) is as of little importance to his work as the fact that a major physicist is not divinely protected from simple errors in calculus; the probability of finding them in his published work is virtually negligible.

But perhaps the most seldom-found qualification for *ijtihad* in our time is the substantive command of the Koran and hadith corpus. In authenticating a ruling connected with a particular hadith, for example, when the person who has related the hadith is an Islamic scholar of the first rank, it is not enough for a student or popular writer to find one chain of transmission for the hadith that is weak. There are a great many hadiths with several chains of transmission, and adequate scholarly treatment of how these affect a hadith's authenticity has been traditionally held to require a hadith master (hafiz), those like al-Bukhari, Muslim, al-Dhahabi, Ibn Kathir, or al-Suyuti who have memorized at least 100,000 hadiths—their texts, chains of transmission, and significance—to undertake the comparative study of the hadith's various chains of transmission that cannot be accurately assessed without such knowledge. Today, when not one hadith master (hafiz) remains in the Muslim Community, we do not accept the judgement of any reclassifiers of hadith, no matter how large their popular following, unless it is corroborated by the work of previous hadith masters.

Other necessary qualifications for *ijtihad* are discussed in the following passage, which details the knowledge that an Islamic judge must have:

8.11.b . . . [To qualifiy as an Islamic judge (qadi), one must:] possess knowledge of the rulings of Sacred Law, meaning by way of personal legal reasoning (ijtihad) from primary texts, not merely by following a particular qualified scholar (taqlid), (i.e. if he follows qualified scholarship, he must know and agree with how the rulings are derived, not merely report them). Being qualified to perform legal reasoning (ijtihad) requires knowledge of the rules and principles of the Koran, the sunna (i.e. hadith), as well as knowledge of scholarly consensus (ijma') and analogy (*qiyas,* def: III below), together with knowing types of each of these.

(I) The types of Koranic rules include, for example:

(1) those ('amm) of general applicability to different types of legal ruling;

(2) those (khass) applicable to only one particular ruling or type of ruling;

(3) those (mujmal) which require details and explanation in order to be properly understood;

(4) those (mubayyan) which are plain without added details;

(5) those (mutlaq) applicable without restriction;

(6) those (muqayyad) which have restrictions;

(7) those (nass) which unequivocally decide a particular legal question;

(8) those (dhahir) with a probable legal signification, but which may also bear an alternative interpretation;

(9) those (nasikh) which supersede previously revealed Koranic verses;

(10) and those (mansukh) which are superseded by later verses.

(II) The types of sunna (n: i.e. hadith) include:

(1) hadiths (mutawatir) related by whole groups of individuals from whole groups, in multiple contiguous channels of transmission leading back to the Prophet himself (Allah bless him and give him peace), such that the sheer number of separate channels at each state of transmission is too many for it to be possible for all to have conspired to fabricate the hadith (which is thereby obligatory to believe in, and the denial of which is unbelief (kufr));

(2) hadiths (ahad) related by fewer than the above-men-

tioned group at one or more stages of the transmission, though traced through contiguous successive narrators back to the Prophet (Allah bless him and give him peace). (n: If a hadith is transmitted through just one individual at any point in the history of its transmission, the hadith is termed *singular* (gharib). If it is transmitted through just *two* people at any stage of its transmission, it is termed *rare* ('aziz). If its channels of transmission come through only three people at any point of its history, it is termed *well-known* (mashhur). These designations do not directly influence the authenticity rating of the hadith, since a *singular* hadith, for example, might be *rigorously authenticated* (sahih), *well authenticated* (hasan)—hadiths of both types being obligatory for a Muslim to believe in, though someone who denies them is merely considered corrupt (fasiq), not an unbeliever (kafir)—or *not well authenticated* (da'if), depending on the reliability ratings of the narrators and other factors weighed and judged by hadith specialists);

(3) and other kinds. (n: Yusuf al-Ardabili mentions the following in his list of qualifications for performing legal reasoning (ijtihad):)

(4) hadiths (mursal) from one of those (tabi'i) who had personally met and studied under one or more of the prophetic Companions (Sahaba) but not the Prophet himself (Allah bless him and give him peace) (n: hadiths reported in the form, "The Prophet said [or did] such and such," without mentioning the Companion who related it directly from the Prophet);

(5) hadiths (musnad) related through a contiguous series of transmitters back to the Prophet (Allah bless him and give him peace);

(6) hadiths (muttasil) related through a contiguous series of transmitters (n: either from the Prophet (Allah bless him and give him peace), such a hadith being termed *ascribed* (marfu'), or else only from one of the Companions, such a hadith being termed *arrested* (mawquf));

(7) hadiths (munqati‘) related through a chain of transmitters of whom one is unknown (n: though if two or more are unknown, it is not considered merely *incontiguous* (munqati‘), but rather *problematic* (mu‘dal));

(8) the positive and negative personal factors (jarh wa ta‘dil) determining the reliability ratings of the individual narrators of a hadith's channel of transmission;

(9) the positions held by the most learned of the Companions (Sahaba) on legal questions, and those of the scholars who came after them;

(10) and on which of these positions there is scholarly consensus (def: b7), and which are differed upon (*Kitab al-anwar li a‘mal al-abrar fi fiqh al-Imam al-Shafi‘i* (9.2), 2.391).

(n: The English glosses and remarks on the meanings of the above hadith terminology are from notes taken by the translator at a lesson with hadith specialist Sheikh Shu‘ayb Arna'ut.)

(III) Types of analogical reasoning (qiyas) include:

(1) making an *a fortiori* analogy between acts p and q, where if p takes a ruling, q is even likelier to take the same ruling. For example, if saying "Uff!" to one's parents is unlawful (n: as at Koran 17:23), one may analogically infer that beating them must also be unlawful;

(2) making an analogy between acts p and q, where if p takes a ruling, one may infer that q is equally likely to take the same ruling. For example, if it is unlawful to wrongfully consume an orphan's property, then it must also be unlawful to destroy his property by burning it up;

(3) and making an analogy between acts p and q, where if p takes a ruling, one may infer that it is likely, though less certain, that q takes the same ruling (n: because of a common feature in the two acts which functions as the basis (‘illa) for the analogy). For example, if usurious gain (riba)

is unlawful in selling wheat (dis: k3.1), then it is also unlawful in selling apples, the basis for the analogy being that both are *food.*

The meaning of *knowledge* of the above matters is (n: for a judge) to know part of what is connected with the Koran, sunna (i.e. hadith), and analogy, not complete knowledge of the Book of Allah, total familiarity with the rules of the sunna, or comprehensive mastery of the rules of analogical reasoning, but rather that which is pertinent to giving judgements in court (though an *absolute* expert in Islamic legal reasoning (mujtahid mutlaq) such as Abu Hanifa, Malik, Shafi'i or Ahmad, is obliged to know what relates to every subject matter in Sacred Law). He must know the reliability ratings of hadith narrators in strength and weakness. When two primary texts seem to conflict, he gives precedence to:

(1) those of particular applicability (khass) over those of general applicability ('amm);

(2) those that take restrictions (muqayyad) over those that do not (mutlaq);

(3) those which unequivocally settle a particular question (nass) over those of merely probabilistic legal significance (dhahir);

(4) those which are literal (muhkam) over those which are figurative (mutashabih);

(5) and those which supersede previous rulings, those with a contiguous channel of transmission, and those with a well-authenticated channel of transmission, over their respective opposites.

He must also have knowledge of the Arabic language, its lexicon, grammar, word morphology, and rhetoric.

He must likewise know the positions of the scholars of Sacred Law regarding their consensus (ijma') and differences, and not contradict their consensus (n: which is unlawful) with his own reasoning.

9

WORKS CITED

ثبت المراجع

9.1 ‘Abidin, Muhammad ‘Ala’ al-Din. *al-Hadiyya al-‘Alā’iyya*. Edited and annotated by Muhammad Sa‘id al-Burhani. Damascus: Dar al-Ma‘arif, 1398/1978.

9.2 al-Ardabili, Yusuf ibn Ibrahim. *Kitāb al-anwār li a‘māl al-abrār fī fiqh al-Imām al-Shāfi‘ī.* Cairo: Mustafa al-Babi al-Halabi, 1326/1908.

9.3 al-‘Azizi, ‘Ali ibn Ahmad, and Jalal al-Din al-Suyuti. *al-Sirāj al-munīr sharḥ al-Jāmi‘ al-saghīr* [a commentary by ‘Azizi on the hadiths of Suyuti’s al-Jami‘ al-saghir]. 3 vols. Cairo: Ahmad al-Babi al-Halabi, 1312/1894–95.

9.4 al-Baghdadi, ‘Abd al-Qahir. *Uṣūl al-dīn.* Istanbul: Matba‘a al-Dawla, 1346/1928.

9.5 al-Buti, Muhammad Sa‘id. *al-Salafiyya marḥala zamaniyya mubāraka lā madhhab Islāmī.* Damascus: Dar al-Fikr, 1408/1988.

9.6 al-Dardir, Ahmad ibn Muhammad, and Ahmad ibn Muhammad al-Sawi. *al-Sharḥ al-saghīr ‘alā Aqrab al-masālik ilā madhhab al-Imām Mālik* [Dardir’s interlineal exegesis of his own *Aqrab al-masālik* printed with it above the commentary of Sawi]. Edited with introduction and appendices by Mustafa Kamal Wasfi. 4 vols. Cairo: Dar al-Ma‘arif, 1394/1974.

9.7 al-Faqir, 'Ali Mustafa. *al-Imām al-'Izz ibn 'Abd al-Salām wa atharuhu fī al-fiqh al-Islāmī*. 2 vols. Amman: Mudiriyya al-Ifta' li al-Quwat al-Musallaha al-Urduniyya, 1399/1979.

9.8 al-Ghazali, Abu Hamid. *Ihyā' 'ulūm al-dīn* [with notes on its hadiths by Zayn al-Din al-'Iraqi printed below it, and 'Umar Suhrawardi's *'Awārif al-ma'ārif* on its margins]. 4 vols. 1347/1929. Reprint. Beirut: 'Alam al-kutub, n.d.

9.9 al-Hashimi, Muhammad ibn Ahmad. *al-Ḥall al-sadīd li mā astashkalahu al-murīd*. Edited with appendices by Muhammad Sa'id al-Burhani. Damascus: Muhammad Sa'id al-Burhani, 1383/1963.

9.10 Ibn 'Ata' Illah, Ahmad ibn Muhammad. *al-Ḥikam al-'Atā'iyya wa al-munājāt al-ilāhiyya*. Damascus: al-Maktaba al-'Arabiyya, 1393/1973.

9.11 al-Jaziri, 'Abd al-Rahman. *al-Fiqh 'alā al-madhāhib al-arba'a*. 5 vols. 1392/1972. Reprint. Beirut: Dar al-Fikr, n.d.

9.12 al-Jurdani, Muhammad ibn 'Abdullah, and Yahya ibn Sharaf al-Nawawi. *al-Jawāhir al-lu'lu'iyya fī sharḥ al-Arba'īn al-Nawawiyya* [the hadiths of Nawawi's *al-Arba'un al-Nawawiyya* printed above Jurdani's commentary]. 1328/1910. Reprint. Damascus: 'Abd al-Wakil al-Durubi, n.d.

9.13 Keller, Nuh Ha Mim, tr. *Reliance of the Traveller* [the Arabic text of Ahmad ibn al-Naqib al-Misri's *'Umdat al-sālik* with facing English translation, notes, and appendices]. Evanston: Sunna Books, 1414/1993.

9.14 Khallaf, 'Abd al-Wahhab. *'Ilm uṣūl al-fiqh*. Kuwait: Dar al-Qalam, 1361/1942.

9.15 al-Maliki, Muhammad al-Hasan ibn 'Alawi. *Mafāhīm yajibu an tuṣaḥḥaḥa*. Dubai: Hashr ibn Muhammad ibn al-Shaykh Ahmad Dalmuk, 1407/1986.

9.16 al-Maydani, 'Abd al-Ghani al-Ghunaymi, and Ahmad ibn Muhammad al-Quduri. *al-Lubāb fī sharḥ al-Kitāb* [Quduri's *al-Kitāb* with Maydani's commentary printed below it]. Edited by Mahmud Amin al-Nawawi and Muhammad Muhyiddin 'Abd al-Hamid. 4 vols. 1399/1979.

9.17 al-Misri, Ahmad ibn al-Naqib. *'Umdat al-sālik wa 'uddat al-nāsik.* 1367/1948. Reprint. Damascus: 'Abd al-Wakil al-Durubi wa Dar al-Karam, n.d.

9.18 Mu'adhdhin, Salih, and Muhammad al-Sabbagh, eds. Introduction and notes to *'Umdat al-sālik wa 'uddat al-nāsik* by Ahmad ibn al-Naqib al-Misri. Damascus: Maktaba al-Ghazali, 1405/1985.

9.19 Muslim ibn al-Hajjaj. *Ṣaḥīḥ Muslim.* Edited and annotated by Muhammad Fu'ad 'Abd al-Baqi. 5 vols. 1376/1956. Reprint. Beirut: Dar al-Fikr, 1403/1983.

9.20 al-Nabahani, Yusuf ibn Isma'il. *Jāmi' karāmāt al-awliyā'.* 2 vols. 1329/1911. Reprint (2 vols. in 1). Beirut: Dar Sadir, n.d.

9.21 al-Nawawi, Yahya ibn Sharaf. *al-Maqāsid fī bayān mā yajibu ma'rifatuhu min al-dīn.* Damascus: Dar al-Iman, 1405/1985.

9.22 al-Nawawi, Yahya ibn Sharaf, Abu Ishaq al-Shirazi, and Taqi al-Din al-Subki. *al-Majmū': sharḥ al-Muhadhdhab* [Shirazi's *al-Muhadhdhab* printed with Nawawi's interlineal commentary, which is completed by Subki's supplement (vols. 10–20) *Takmila al-Majmū'*]. 20 vols. N.d. Reprint. Medina: al-Maktaba al-Salafiyya, n.d.

9.23 al-Rifa'i, Yusuf al-Sayyid Hashim. *Adilla Ahl al-Sunna wa al-Jamā'a aw al-Radd al-muḥkam al-manī' 'alā munkarāt wa shubuhāt Ibn Manī' fī tahajjumihi 'alā al-Sayyid Muḥammad 'Alawī al-Māliki al-Makkī.* Kuwait: Dar al-Siyasa, 1404/1984.

9.24 al-Shadhili, Muhammad Abu al-Muwahib, Ahmad

ibn Muhammad al-Sharishi, and Ahmad ibn Ahmad Zarruq. *Kitāb qawānīn ḥukm al-ishrāq ilā kāffa al-Ṣufiyya fī jamī' al-afāq* [containing Shadhili's *Qawānīn* followed by Sharishi's poem *Anwār al-sarā'ir wa sarā'ir al-anwār* and Zarruq's *Uṣūl al-ṭarīqa al-Shādhiliyya*]. Damascus: 'Abd al-Wakil al-Durubi, 1386/1986.

9.25 al-Sha'rani, *al-Ṭabaqāt al-kubrā al-musamma bi Lawāqih al-anwār fī ṭabāqāt al-akhyār*. 2 vols. 1374/1954. Reprint (2 vols. in 1). Beirut: Dar al-Fikr, n.d.

10

ARABIC SUPPLICATIONS AND DHIKR

أدعية وأذكار

10.1 (1.5) أَشْهَدُ أَنْ لَا إِلٰهَ إِلَّا ٱللهُ وَأَشْهَدُ أَنَّ مُحَمَّداً رَسُولُ ٱللهِ.

10.2 (1.12) أَشْهَدُ أَنْ لَا إِلٰهَ إِلَّا ٱللهُ وَأَشْهَدُ أَنَّ مُحَمَّداً رَسُولُ ٱللهِ

10.3 (1.14) لَا إِلٰهَ إِلَّا ٱللهُ.

10.4 (1.14, second par.) سُبْحَانَكَ لَا نُحْصِي ثَنَاءً عَلَيْكَ أَنْتَ كَمَا أَثْنَيْتَ عَلَى نَفْسِكَ.

10.5 (1.14, third par.) الحَمْدُ لِلهِ حَمْداً يُوَافِي نِعَمَهُ وَيُكَافِيءُ مَزِيدَه.

10.6 (1.14, fourth par.) اَللّٰهُمَّ صَلِّ عَلَى مُحَمَّدٍ وَعَلَى آلِ مُحَمَّدٍ كَمَا صَلَّيْتَ عَلَى إِبْرَاهِيمَ وَعَلَى آلِ إِبْرَاهِيمَ وَبَارِكْ عَلَى مُحَمَّدٍ وَعَلَى آلِ مُحَمَّدٍ كَمَا بَارَكْتَ عَلَى إِبْرَاهِيمَ وَعَلَى آلِ إِبْرَاهِيمَ فِي العَالَمِينَ إِنَّكَ حَمِيدٌ مَجِيد.

10.7 (2.11(1)) بِسْمِ ٱللهِ الرَّحْمٰنِ الرَّحِيم.

10.8 (3.9) اَللهُ أَكْبَر.

10.9 (3.9, end) اَلسَّلَامُ عَلَيْكُم.

10.10 (3.10(1)) اَللهُ أَكْبَر.

10.11 (3.10(3)) وَجَّهْتُ وَجْهِي لِلَّذِي فَطَرَ ٱلسَّمٰوَاتِ وَٱلأَرْضَ وَمَا أَنَا مِنَ المُشْرِكِينَ إِنَّ صَلَاتِي وَنُسُكِي وَمَحْيَايَ وَمَمَاتِي لِلهِ رَبِّ العَالَمِينَ لَا شَرِيكَ لَهُ وَبِذٰلِكَ أُمِرْتُ وَأَنَا مِنَ المُسلِمِين.

10.12 (3.10(4)) أَعُوذُ بِاللهِ مِنَ الشَّيْطَانِ الرَّجِيمِ.

10.13 (3.10(5)) بِسْمِ ٱللَّهِ ٱلرَّحْمَٰنِ ٱلرَّحِيمِ ٱلْحَمْدُ لِلَّهِ
رَبِّ ٱلْعَٰلَمِينَ ٱلرَّحْمَٰنِ ٱلرَّحِيمِ مَٰلِكِ يَوْمِ ٱلدِّينِ إِيَّاكَ نَعْبُدُ وَإِيَّاكَ نَسْتَعِينُ
ٱهْدِنَا ٱلصِّرَٰطَ ٱلْمُسْتَقِيمَ صِرَٰطَ ٱلَّذِينَ أَنْعَمْتَ عَلَيْهِمْ غَيْرِ ٱلْمَغْضُوبِ عَلَيْهِمْ وَلَا
ٱلضَّآلِّينَ

10.14 (3.10(5), end) آمين .

10.15 (3.10(6), second par.) قُلْ هُوَ ٱللَّهُ أَحَدٌ ٱللَّهُ ٱلصَّمَدُ لَمْ يَلِدْ
وَلَمْ يُولَدْ وَلَمْ يَكُن لَّهُۥ كُفُوًا أَحَدٌۢ

10.16 (3.10(6), third par.) قُلْ أَعُوذُ بِرَبِّ ٱلْفَلَقِ مِن شَرِّ مَا خَلَقَ وَمِن شَرِّ
غَاسِقٍ إِذَا وَقَبَ وَمِن شَرِّ ٱلنَّفَّٰثَٰتِ فِى ٱلْعُقَدِ وَمِن شَرِّ حَاسِدٍ إِذَا حَسَدَ

10.17 (3.10(6), fourth par.) قُلْ أَعُوذُ بِرَبِّ ٱلنَّاسِ مَلِكِ ٱلنَّاسِ إِلَٰهِ ٱلنَّاسِ
مِن شَرِّ ٱلْوَسْوَاسِ ٱلْخَنَّاسِ ٱلَّذِى يُوَسْوِسُ فِى صُدُورِ ٱلنَّاسِ مِنَ ٱلْجِنَّةِ
وَٱلنَّاسِ

10.18 (3.10(7)) سُبْحَانَ رَبِّيَ الْعَظِيم .

10.19 (3.10(8)) سَمِعَ اللهُ لِمَنْ حَمِدَه .

10.20 (3.10(8)) رَبَّنَا لَكَ الحَمْد .

10.21 (3.10(8)) مِلْءَ السَّمٰواتِ وَمِلْءَ الأَرْضِ وَمِلْءَ مَا شِئْتَ مِنْ شَيْءٍ
بَعْد .

10.22 (3.10(9)) سُبْحَانَ رَبِّيَ الْأَعْلَى .

10.23 (3.10(10)) أَللّهُمَّ آغْفِرْ لِي وَآرْحَمْنِي وَعَافِنِي وَآجْبُرْنِي وَآهْدِنِي
وَآرْزُقْنِي .

10.24 (3.10(15)) اَلتَّحِيَّاتُ المُبارَكَاتُ الصَّلَوَاتُ الطَّيِّبَاتُ لله السَّلاَمُ عَلَيْكَ
أَيُّهَا النَّبِيُّ وَرَحْمَةُ آللهِ وَبَرَكَاتُهُ السَّلاَمُ عَلَيْنَا وَعَلَى عِبَادِ آللهِ الصَّالِحِينَ أَشْهَدُ أَنْ
لاَ إِلـهَ إِلاَّ آللهُ وَأَشْهَدُ أَنَّ مُحَمَّداً رَسُولُ آلله .

10.25 (3.10(16)) اَللّهُمَّ صَلِّ عَلَى سَيِّدِنا مُحَمَّد .

10.26 (3.10(16)) اَللّهُمَّ صَلِّ عَلَى سَيِّدِنا مُحَمَّدٍ وَعَلَى آلِ سَيِّدِنا مُحَمَّدٍ
كَمَا صَلَّيْتَ عَلَى سَيِّدِنا إِبْرَاهِيمَ وَعَلَى آلِ سَيِّدِنا إِبْرَاهِيمَ وَبارِكْ عَلَى سَيِّدِنا مُحَمَّدٍ
وَعَلَى آلِ سَيِّدِنا مُحَمَّدٍ كَمَا بَارَكْتَ عَلَى سَيِّدِنا إِبْرَاهِيمَ وَعَلَى آلِ سَيِّدِنا إِبْرَاهِيمَ

فِي العَالَمِينَ إِنَّكَ حَمِيدٌ مَجِيد.

10.27 (3.10(17)) اَلسَّلَامُ عَلَيْكُمْ وَرَحْمَةُ آللهِ.

10.28 (3.11(d)) بِسْمِ آللهِ الرَّحْمٰنِ الرَّحِيمِ.

10.29 (3.12(e)) اَللّٰهُمَّ آهْدِنَا فِيمَنْ هَدَيْتَ وَعَافِنَا فِيمَنْ عَافَيْتَ وَتَوَلَّنَا فِيمَنْ تَوَلَّيْتَ وَبَارِكْ لَنَا فِيمَا أَعْطَيْتَ وَقِنَا شَرَّ مَا قَضَيْتَ فَإِنَّكَ تَقْضِي وَلَا يُقْضَى عَلَيْكَ وَإِنَّهُ لَا يَذِلُّ مَنْ وَالَيْتَ وَلَا يَعِزُّ مَنْ عَادَيْتَ. تَبَارَكْتَ رَبَّنَا وَتَعَالَيْتَ.

10.30 (3.24(2)) اَلْحَمْدُ لِلّٰهِ.

10.31 (3.24(7)) إِنَّ الحَمْدَ لِلّٰهِ نَحْمَدُهُ نَسْتَعِينُهُ وَنَسْتَغْفِرُهُ وَنَعُوذُ بِاللهِ مِنْ شُرُورِ أَنْفُسِنَا وَمِنْ سَيِّئَاتِ أَعْمَالِنَا. مَنْ يَهْدِهِ آللهُ فَلَا مُضِلَّ لَهُ، وَمَنْ يُضْلِلْ فَلَا هَادِيَ لَهُ وَأَشْهَدُ أَنْ لَا إِلٰهَ إِلَّا آللهُ وَحْدَهُ لَا شَرِيكَ لَهُ وَأَشْهَدُ أَنَّ مُحَمَّداً عَبْدُهُ وَرَسُولُهُ صَلَّى آللهُ عَلَيْهِ وَسَلَّمَ وَعَلَى آلِهِ وَأَصْحَابِهِ.

10.32 (3.24(7)) يَٰٓأَيُّهَا ٱلنَّاسُ ٱتَّقُوا۟ رَبَّكُمُ ٱلَّذِى خَلَقَكُم مِّن نَّفْسٍ وَٰحِدَةٍ وَخَلَقَ مِنْهَا زَوْجَهَا وَبَثَّ مِنْهُمَا رِجَالًا كَثِيرًا وَنِسَآءً ۚ وَٱتَّقُوا۟ ٱللَّهَ ٱلَّذِى تَسَآءَلُونَ بِهِۦ وَٱلْأَرْحَامَ ۚ إِنَّ ٱللَّهَ كَانَ عَلَيْكُمْ رَقِيبًا

10.33 (3.24(8)) اَللّٰهُمَّ آغْفِرْ لِلْمُؤْمِنِينَ وَالْمُؤْمِنَاتِ.

10.34 (3.26) سُبْحَانَ آللهِ وَالْحَمْدُ لِلّٰهِ وَلَا إِلٰهَ إِلَّا آللهُ وَآللهُ أَكْبَر.

10.35 (3.26, sixth par.) اَللهُ أَكْبَرُ آللهُ أَكْبَرُ آللهُ أَكْبَرُ لَا إِلٰهَ إِلَّا آللهُ. اَللهُ أَكْبَرُ آللهُ أَكْبَرُ وَلِلّٰهِ الْحَمْدُ وَآللهُ أَكْبَرُ كَبِيراً وَآلحَمْدُ لِلّٰهِ كَثِيراً وَسُبْحَانَ آللهِ بُكْرَةً وَأَصِيلاً، لَا إِلٰهَ إِلَّا آللهُ وَلَا نَعْبُدُ إِلَّا إِيَّاهُ مُخْلِصِينَ لَهُ الدِّينَ وَلَوْ كَرِهَ الْكَافِرُونَ. لَا إِلٰهَ إِلَّا آللهُ وَحْدَهُ، صَدَقَ وَعْدَهُ، وَنَصَرَ عَبْدَهُ وَأَعَزَّ جُنْدَهُ وَهَزَمَ آلْأَحْزَابَ وَحْدَهُ، لَا إِلٰهَ إِلَّا آللهُ وَآللهُ أَكْبَر.

10.36 (3.28) أَسْتَغْفِرُ آللهَ العَظِيمَ الَّذِي لَا إِلٰهَ إِلَّا هُوَ الحَيَّ القَيُّومَ وَأَتُوبُ إِلَيْهِ.

10.37 (3.31) اَللّٰهُمَّ آغْفِرْ لِهَذَا المَيِّت.

10.38 (6.5(3)) لَبَّيْكَ اللّٰهُمَّ لَبَّيْكَ، لَبَّيْكَ لَا شَرِيكَ لَكَ لَبَّيْكَ، إِنَّ الحَمْدَ وَالنِّعْمَةَ لَكَ وَالمُلْكَ، لَا شَرِيكَ لَكَ.

10.39 (7.5(1)) اَللّٰهُمَّ بِكَ نُصْبِحُ وَبِكَ نُمْسِي وَبِكَ نَحْيَا وَبِكَ نَمُوتُ وَإِلَيْكَ النُّشُور.

10.40 (7.5(1)) إِلَيْكَ المَصِير

10.41 (7.5(2)) أَصْبَحْنَا وَأَصْبَحَ الْمُلْكُ لِلهِ وَالحَمْدُ لِلهِ وَالكِبْرِيَاءُ لِلهِ وَالعَظَمَةُ
لِلهِ وَالخَلْقُ وَالأَمْرُ وَاللَّيْلُ وَالنَّهَارُ وَمَا سَكَنَ فِيهِمَا لِلهِ .

10.42 (7.5(3)) اَللّٰهُمَّ مَا أَصْبَحَ بِي مِنْ نِعْمَةٍ أَوْ بِأَحَدٍ مِنْ خَلْقِكَ فَمِنْكَ
وَحْدَكَ لَا شَرِيكَ لَكَ فَلَكَ ٱلحَمْدُ وَلَكَ الشُّكْر.

10.43 (7.5(4)) اَللّٰهُمَّ إِنِّي أَصْبَحْتُ أُشْهِدُكَ وَأُشْهِدُ حَمَلَةَ عَرْشِكَ وَمَلَائِكَتَكَ
وَجَمِيعَ خَلْقِكَ أَنَّكَ أَنْتَ ٱللهُ لَا إِلٰهَ إِلَّا أَنْتَ وَحْدَكَ لَا شَرِيكَ لَكَ وَأَنَّ مُحَمَّداً
عَبْدُكَ وَرَسُولُك .

10.44 (7.5(5)) رَضِيتُ بِاللهِ رَبّاً وَبِالإِسْلَامِ دِيناً وَبِسَيِّدِنَا مُحَمَّدٍ صَلَّى ٱللهُ
عَلَيْهِ وَسَلَّمَ نَبِيّاً وَرَسُولاً .

10.45 (7.5(6)) ءَامَنَ ٱلرَّسُولُ بِمَآ أُنزِلَ إِلَيْهِ مِن رَّبِّهِۦ وَٱلْمُؤْمِنُونَ ۚ كُلٌّ ءَامَنَ بِٱللَّهِ
وَمَلَٰٓئِكَتِهِۦ وَكُتُبِهِۦ وَرُسُلِهِۦ لَا نُفَرِّقُ بَيْنَ أَحَدٍ مِّن رُّسُلِهِۦ ۚ وَقَالُوا۟ سَمِعْنَا وَأَطَعْنَا ۖ غُفْرَانَكَ
رَبَّنَا وَإِلَيْكَ ٱلْمَصِيرُ لَا يُكَلِّفُ ٱللَّهُ نَفْسًا إِلَّا وُسْعَهَا ۚ لَهَا مَا كَسَبَتْ وَعَلَيْهَا مَا ٱكْتَسَبَتْ ۗ
رَبَّنَا لَا تُؤَاخِذْنَآ إِن نَّسِينَآ أَوْ أَخْطَأْنَا ۚ رَبَّنَا وَلَا تَحْمِلْ عَلَيْنَآ إِصْرًا كَمَا حَمَلْتَهُۥ عَلَى
ٱلَّذِينَ مِن قَبْلِنَا ۚ رَبَّنَا وَلَا تُحَمِّلْنَا مَا لَا طَاقَةَ لَنَا بِهِۦ ۖ وَٱعْفُ عَنَّا وَٱغْفِرْ لَنَا وَٱرْحَمْنَآ ۚ أَنتَ
مَوْلَىٰنَا فَٱنصُرْنَا عَلَى ٱلْقَوْمِ ٱلْكَٰفِرِينَ

10.46 (7.5(7)) فَإِن تَوَلَّوْا۟ فَقُلْ حَسْبِىَ ٱللَّهُ لَآ إِلَٰهَ إِلَّا هُوَ ۖ عَلَيْهِ تَوَكَّلْتُ ۖ وَهُوَ
رَبُّ ٱلْعَرْشِ ٱلْعَظِيمِ

10.47 (7.5(8)) فَسُبْحَٰنَ ٱللَّهِ حِينَ تُمْسُونَ وَحِينَ تُصْبِحُونَ وَلَهُ ٱلْحَمْدُ فِى
ٱلسَّمَٰوَٰتِ وَٱلْأَرْضِ وَعَشِيًّا وَحِينَ تُظْهِرُونَ يُخْرِجُ ٱلْحَىَّ مِنَ ٱلْمَيِّتِ وَيُخْرِجُ ٱلْمَيِّتَ مِنَ ٱلْحَىِّ
وَيُحْىِ ٱلْأَرْضَ بَعْدَ مَوْتِهَا ۚ وَكَذَٰلِكَ تُخْرَجُونَ

10.48 (7.5(10)) أَعُوذُ بِاللهِ السَّمِيعِ العَلِيمِ مِنَ الشَّيْطَانِ الرَّجِيمِ .

10.49 (7.5(11)) لَوْ أَنزَلْنَا هَٰذَا ٱلْقُرْءَانَ عَلَىٰ جَبَلٍ لَّرَأَيْتَهُۥ خَٰشِعًا مُّتَصَدِّعًا مِّنْ
خَشْيَةِ ٱللَّهِ ۚ وَتِلْكَ ٱلْأَمْثَٰلُ نَضْرِبُهَا لِلنَّاسِ لَعَلَّهُمْ يَتَفَكَّرُونَ هُوَ ٱللَّهُ ٱلَّذِى لَآ إِلَٰهَ إِلَّا هُوَ ۖ
عَٰلِمُ ٱلْغَيْبِ وَٱلشَّهَٰدَةِ ۖ هُوَ ٱلرَّحْمَٰنُ ٱلرَّحِيمُ هُوَ ٱللَّهُ ٱلَّذِى لَآ إِلَٰهَ إِلَّا هُوَ ٱلْمَلِكُ
ٱلْقُدُّوسُ ٱلسَّلَٰمُ ٱلْمُؤْمِنُ ٱلْمُهَيْمِنُ ٱلْعَزِيزُ ٱلْجَبَّارُ ٱلْمُتَكَبِّرُ ۚ سُبْحَٰنَ ٱللَّهِ عَمَّا
يُشْرِكُونَ هُوَ ٱللَّهُ ٱلْخَٰلِقُ ٱلْبَارِئُ ٱلْمُصَوِّرُ ۖ لَهُ ٱلْأَسْمَآءُ ٱلْحُسْنَىٰ ۚ يُسَبِّحُ لَهُۥ مَا فِى ٱلسَّمَٰوَٰتِ
وَٱلْأَرْضِ ۖ وَهُوَ ٱلْعَزِيزُ ٱلْحَكِيمُ

10.50 (7.5(13)) بِسْمِ ٱللهِ ٱلَّذِي لَا يَضُرُّ مَعَ ٱسْمِهِ شَيْءٌ فِي الأَرْضِ وَلَا
فِي السَّمَاءِ وَهُوَ السَّمِيعُ العَلِيم.

10.51 (7.5(14)) أَعُـوذُ بِكَلِمَاتِ ٱللهِ ٱلتَّامَّاتِ مِنْ غَضَبِهِ وَعِقَابِهِ وَشَرِّ عِبَادِهِ
وَمِنْ هَمَزَاتِ ٱلشَّيَاطِينَ وَأَنْ يَحْضُرُونِ.

10.52 (7.5(15)) اَسْتَغْفِرُ ٱللهَ العَظِيمَ الَّذِي لَا إِلٰـهَ إِلَّا هُوَ الحَيَّ القَيُّومَ وَأَتُوبُ
إِلَيْه.

10.53 (7.5(16)) سُبْحَانَ ٱللهِ وَبِحَمْدِه.

10.54 (7.5(17)) سُبْحَـانَ ٱللهِ وَبِحَمْدِهِ عَدَدَ خَلْقِهِ وَرِضَا نَفْسِهِ وَزِنَةَ عَرْشِهِ
وَمِدَادَ كَلِمَاتِه.

10.55 (7.5(18)) سُبْحَانَ ٱللهِ وَالحَمْدُ لِلهِ وَلَا إِلٰـهَ إِلَّا ٱللهُ وَٱللهُ أَكْبَر.

10.56 (7.5(19)) لَا حَوْلَ وَلَا قُوَّةَ إِلَّا بِاللهِ العَلِيِّ العَظِيم.

10.57 (7.5(20)) لَا إِلٰـهَ إِلَّا ٱللهُ المَلِكُ الحَقُّ المُبِين.

10.58 (7.5(21)) لَا إِلٰـهَ إِلَّا ٱللهُ وَحْدَهُ لَا شَرِيكَ لَهُ، لَهُ المُلْكُ وَلَهُ الحَمْدُ
وَهُوَ عَلَى كُلِّ شَيْءٍ قَدِير.

10.59 (7.5(22)) اَللّٰهُمَّ صَلِّ عَلَى سَيِّدِنَا مُحَمَّدٍ عَبْدِكَ وَنَبِيِّكَ وَحَبِيبِكَ النَّبِيِّ
الأُمِّيِّ وَعَلَى آلِهِ وَصَحْبِهِ وَسَلِّم.

IMAM NAWAWI

Imam Nawawi is Yahya ibn Sharaf ibn Murri ibn Hasan, Abu Zakariyya Muhyi al-Din al-Nawawi, born in the village of Nawa on the Horan Plain of southern Syria in 631/1233. He was the Imam of the late Shafi'i school, the scholar of his time in knowledge, piety, and abstinence, a hadith master (hafiz), biographer, lexicologist, and a saintly mystic who is generally considered to have been a friend of Allah (wali).

When he first came to Damascus in A.H. 649, he memorized the text of Abu Ishaq Shirazi's *al-Tanbīh* [The notification] in four and a half months, then the first quarter of Shirazi's *al-Muhadhdhab* [The rarefaction], after which he accompanied his father on hajj, then visited Medina, and then returned to Damascus, where he assiduously devoted himself to mastering the Islamic sciences. He learned Shafi'i jurisprudence, hadith, tenets of faith, fundamentals of Islamic law, Arabic, and other subjects from more than twenty-two scholars of the time, including Abu Ibrahim Ishaq al-Maghribi, 'Abd al-Rahman ibn Qudama al-Maqdisi, and others, at a period of his life in which, as his biographer Imam Dhahabi was to note, "his dedication to learning, night and day, became proverbial." Spending all his time either worshipping or gaining Sacred Knowledge, he took some twelve lessons a day, only dozed off at night in moments when sleep overcome him, and drilled himself in the lessons he learned by heart even while walking along the street.

Fastidious in detail and deep in understanding of the subjects he thus mastered, he authored many famous works in Islamic jurisprudence, hadith, history, and legal opinion, among the best known of which are his *Minhāj al-ṭālibīn* [The seeker's road], which has become a main reference for the Shafi'i school, *Riyāḍ al-ṣāliḥīn* [The gardens of the righteous] and *Kitāb al-adhkār* [The book of the remembrances of Allah] in hadith, as well as his eighteen-volume *Sharḥ Ṣaḥīḥ Muslim* [Commentary on Muslim's "Sahih"], which he was the first to divide into chapters and give headings describing its content.

He lived the life of those dedicated to the hereafter, ate simply, and it is related that his entire wardrobe consisted of a turban and an ankle-length shirt (thawb) with a single button at the collar.

After a residence in Damascus of twenty-seven years spent in devotion to Allah; learning, teaching, and authoring his famous and enduring works, he returned the books he had borrowed from charitable endowments, bade his friends farewell, visited the graves of his sheikhs who had died, and departed, going first to Jerusalem and then to his native Nawa, where he became ill at his father's home and died at the age of forty-four in 676/1277, young in years but great in benefit to the Islamic Community. Perhaps it was because of his tremendous sincerity that Allah gave him such success in his written works, for it is difficult to name an Islamic figure of the last seven centuries whose books have enjoyed a wider popularity or been more treasured and frequently used by Muslims in all parts the Islamic world than this pure-hearted scholar.

THE ORIGIN OF THE TEXT

The specialist in Arabic books in manuscript and print al-Zirikli lists *al-Maqāsid* among Nawawi's works in his *al-A'lām* (8 vols. Beirut: Dar al-'Ilm li al-Milayin, 1405/1984, 8.149). The *Maqāsid* has been printed, under various titles and subtitles, some five times in Cairo, Beirut, and Damascus in the present century. It also exists in two handwritten manuscripts known to the translator: *Maqāsid li al-Nawawī* (Manuscript: 22 fols. Undated. Number 1471, al-Zahiriyya, Maktaba al-Asad, Damascus); and *al-Maqāsid* (Manuscript: 31 fols. 1187/1773. Private collection of Iyad al-Tabba', Damascus).

Although the book is not listed among al-Nawawi's works by early biographers such as Ibn al-'Attar (d. 724/1324), Sakhkhawi (902/1497), and Suyuti (911/1505), this is not particularly strange, firstly in view of the work's relative importance and brevity (twenty-two pages in manuscript) compared to, for example, Nawawi's *Sharḥ al-Muhadhdhab* (twenty volumes in print) or *Sharḥ Ṣaḥīḥ Muslim* (eighteen volumes), or *Rawḍa al-ṭālibīn* (twelve volumes) in relation to which it is only a small *matn;* and secondly because the biographers were not exhaustive. Ibn al-'Attar, Suyuti tells us, "did not list all [of Nawawi's works], or even come close" (*al-Minhāj al-sawī.* Beirut: Dar Ibn Hazm, 1408/1988, 65). Suyuti himself names thirty-three works, which are "what comes to my mind of his works, after checking" (ibid.), while Sakhkhawi says that Nawawi authored "about fifty works" (*al-Manhal al-'adhb al-rawī.* Medina: Maktaba Dar al-Turath, 1409/1989, 63), though he only names forty of them. Their not mentioning *al-Maqāsid* would not seem to be an objection to the authenticity of the manuscript copies, without other internal textual evidence.

As for this content, the tenets of faith ('aqida) at the first of the book are those of orthodox Islam, which Imam Nawawi ably represents, and are in complete agreement with his positions on tenets of faith in the introduction to *Sharḥ al-Muhadhdhab* and many places in his *Sharḥ Ṣaḥīḥ Muslim.* The main body of the book, as will not be lost on anyone familiar with Shafi'i fiqh, is a summary of the legal rulings found in Nawawi's *Minhāj al-ṭālibīn* and other famous works in Islamic jurisprudence.

The final section on Sufism is consonant not only with the way Imam Nawawi lived and was, but with his book on the subject *Bustān al-'ārifīn* [The grove of the knowers of Allah], as well as the many passages in his introduction to *Sharḥ al-Muhadhdhab* and throughout his *Kitāb al-adhkār* that are quoted from Qushayri's manual of Sufism *al-Risāla al-Qushayriyya.* Although the principles that appear in this final section were given with only slight differences by later author Ahmad Zarruq (d. 899/1493) in answer to a question about the fundamentals of Sufism (*Qawānīn ḥukm al-ishrāq.* Damascus: Abd al-Wakil Durubi, 1386/1966, 117–19), Zarruq's version is exposited in greater detail, quotes other Sufis, and is more than twice as long as the *Maqāsid*'s version, sufficient by the standards of the times to be presented as his own without reference to previous sources. More tellingly perhaps, *principles* of a traditional discipline mean those that are known and adhered to by all who share in it, and cannot be regarded as the ideas of a particular author.

To summarize, while early biographers do not mention the present *matn* by name, their lists of the author's works are not complete, and the content of the *Maqāsid* that bears the name of Imam Nawawi in manuscript copies and contemporary printed versions is attested to by his many other writings on tenets of faith, jurisprudence, and Sufism. With its small size, it is one of the most useful manuals of Islamic personal law available, and is likely to remain so.